HOW

TV

CHANGED

AMERICA'S

MIND

HOW TV CHANGED AMERICA'S MIND

BY EDWARD WAKIN

LOTHROP, LEE & SHEPARD BOOKS
NEW YORK

Photo credit page 2-3: American Family Watching TV Together, June 25, 1957. (Library of Congress)

Special thanks to Sears, Robuck and Co. for permission to use images from the Fall/Winter 1955, Winter Sale 1963, Fall/Winter 1979, Spring/Summer 1987, and Spring/Summer 1991 Sears catalogs in the original artwork by William Cotton on pages 16-17, 54-55, 102-103, 140-141, and 180-181, respectively. The art on pages 12 and 231 is a composite of images from all five catalogs.

Printed in the United States of America.
First Edition   1 2 3 4 5 6 7 8 9 10
Library of Congress Cataloging in Publication Data
Wakin, Edward. How TV changed America's mind / by Edward Wakin
p.   cm. ISBN 0-688-13482-3. 1. Television broadcasting of news—
United States—Juvenile literature. [1. Television broadcasting of news.]
I. Title. PN4888.T4W35 1995 070.1'95—dc20
94-22542 CIP AC

TO MY GRANDSON
THOMAS

𝓟𝓐𝓡𝓣 2

THE 1960s

PART 3

THE 1970s

PART 4
THE 1980s

PART 5
THE 1990s

HOW
TV
CHANGED
AMERICA'S
MIND

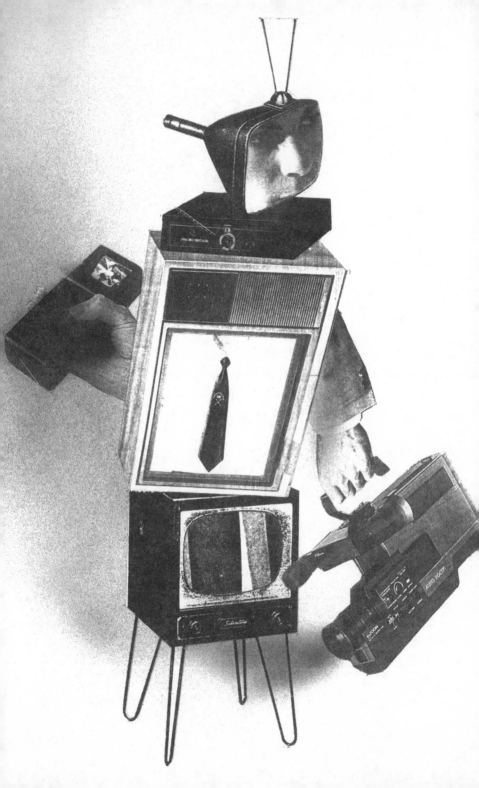

" A TELEVISION REVOLUTION "

Once upon a time—in the year 1946—there were only seven thousand TV sets in the United States. Americans still tuned in to radio as the nation's town crier.

TV started out as a special guest in a few privileged homes. In 1948, when the celebrated journalist Theodore H. White left the United States to work abroad, he had never visited a private home that had a TV set. When he returned five years later in 1953, he was stunned by what he called "a television revolution."

In no time at all, Americans became glued to the TV set in the living room. Media analyst Jeff Greenfield summed up what had happened: "In the early 1950s, by the millions, we took television into our homes and closed the door behind us." The special guest took over.

Americans now watch television the way fish swim in water. They take it for granted. Television news and public affairs programs present history in the making and in the process shape the way Americans think, feel, and react. In the second half of the twentieth century, almost everybody watches TV. Ninety-eight percent of all U.S. households have at least one color TV set. On average, Americans watch TV one out of every four waking hours. At peak moments the whole nation watches together.

TV has become a lifetime companion from the cradle to the grave. By 1992, boys and girls between two and five years old watched TV twenty-five and one-half hours each week. Men over fifty-five watched about thirty-eight and one-half hours a week, women that age watched more than forty-four hours a week.

Looking back at the United States before and after television, historian William Manchester called television "a great, silent agent of change." Television changed the face and the pace of politics. It changed attitudes toward war. It magnified heroes and exposed villains. It brought confrontations into the living room. It also opened eyes by calling attention to situations that otherwise would have remained out of sight.

These effects of TV stood out in five recurring categories: Confrontation, Politics, War, Heroes and Villains, and Eye-Openers. This book tells the story of how TV worked to change America's mind in each category, decade by decade.

Commentators have groped for ways to describe what happened because of TV. The poet Carl Sandburg ended up saying that "the impact of television on our culture is just indescribable." He compared it to the invention of printing.

A close look at that impact is fascinating as history and revealing about television. It recalls and illuminates major events in the second half of the twentieth century. It also helps Americans understand TV as a major force in their lives. Otherwise, viewers watch television's instant history with their eyes "closed."

TV—too big, too important, too powerful to ignore—is a window on the world, a magnifier of events, a screen that commands the entire country to pay attention. It is what Americans rely on to find out about the world. They can't do without it from the time they get up in the morning to the time they go to bed. They can't imagine life without TV telling them what's happening.

A man who had just received an artificial heart summed it up best. As nurses removed tubes draining his chest after the operation, he asked them to turn on the television. He explained why: "I want to see whether I'm alive and how well I'm doing."

1
THE 1950s:

" NOBODY IS MAD WITH NOBODY "

The United States was the right place and the 1950s the right time to launch the Age of Television.

The nation had emerged from World War II not only victorious but an economic powerhouse. While bombers had flattened the factories of Europe, U.S. factories were untouched. By the 1950s, they were producing half of the goods and services in the entire world.

Americans, for their part, were eager to buy what their factories produced, and TV had unprecedented ability to sell. From toys to toothpaste, from candy bars to cars—you name it—television sold them to a country with the world's highest standard of living.

Not surprisingly, American consumers felt good about themselves and their country. In 1955, *Life* magazine described the United States as "a nation up to its ears in domestic tranquility . . . embroiled in no war, impeded by no major strikes, blessed by almost full employment." The magazine's memorable headline proclaimed: "Nobody Is Mad with Nobody."

Dwight D. Eisenhower, the hero-general who had directed the victorious Allied invasion of Europe in World War II, was the kind of reassuring leader that Americans wanted. He was a father figure whose popularity was summed up in the political slogan based on his nickname: "I Like Ike." An Eisenhower era of prosperity dominated his two terms as U.S. president from 1953 to 1961.

TV went all out to entertain the Silent Generation, called that because of the way they accepted the status quo. Why not? They had a good deal. By the end of the decade, their personal income had increased by 50 percent.

There was a stampede to buy televisions at the rate of 5 million sets each year. By 1953, Americans owned more TV sets than bathtubs. By 1954, the frozen TV dinner made it possible to eat and watch at the same time. By 1955, 88 percent of all homes had at least one set, and Americans watched an average of four to five hours a day.

Something else happened on TV. Besides distracting Americans with entertainment, TV opened a window on the world. As early as September 4, 1951, about 40 million people saw their first coast-to-coast TV broadcast over ninety-four stations. It was President Harry S. Truman's address at the Japanese Peace Treaty Conference in San Francisco.

However, as Americans basked in World War II victory and postwar prosperity, the world was still a dangerous place. A cold war pitted the world's two superpowers, the United States and the Soviet Union, against each other. It was a worldwide war of propaganda, power politics, subversion, and spying, punctuated by a shooting war on the Korean peninsula in East Asia.

With nuclear weapons on both sides, a hot, all-out war between the United States and the Soviet Union was out of the question. It could destroy humankind as TV showed Americans in reporting on the hydrogen bomb.

The first H-bomb test by the United States took place in November 1952, and a film of the test was released sixteen months later. It showed the H-bomb blowing an island out of the Pacific Ocean. Such was the power of the H-bomb that it could reduce an entire city to ashes.

"Television viewers," *Life* magazine reported, "knew they were in an awesome new chapter in man's history."

On the home front, America confronted a historic May 17, 1954, decision by the U.S. Supreme Court. By a unanimous vote, the Court declared that racial segregation in public schools was unconstitutional. Segregation meant inequality for African-American students and denied them equal protection under the law. The Supreme Court had spoken, and it was up to the seventeen states with racially segregated schools to comply by acting to end school segregation. TV would show what happened.

The same audience that rushed to the home screen for entertainment and escape in the 1950s was also presented with harsh domestic and international realities. TV news and public affairs programs shattered the calm in the living room.

2

1950s CONFRONTATION:

" POSITIVELY THE MOST WONDERFUL THING I EVER SAW "

THE KEFAUVER COMMITTEE HEARINGS

During the week of March 12, 1951, thousands of people stayed home from work. High schools and universities canceled classes. Department stores, ready and waiting for pre-Easter shoppers, were practically deserted.

In Detroit, hardly anyone made phone calls during what was usually the busiest time of day. In New York, vacant cabs roamed the streets looking for passengers, and in the evening most theatergoers didn't show up. An estimated one out of five New Yorkers changed his or her daily routine.

America's most powerful publication, *Life* magazine, reported: "The U.S. and the world had never experienced anything like it."

What Americans experienced was their first blockbuster television event. *Life* called it "the first big television broadcast of an affair of their government, the broadcast from which all future use of television in public affairs must date. . . . Never before had the atten-

Frank Costello's hands shown on television as he testifies before the Kefauver Committee, March 13, 1951. (Top photo: Sam Goldstein, AP/Wide World. Center and bottom photos: UPI/Bettmann)

tion of the nation been riveted so completely on a single matter."

The "single matter" was the criminal underworld and its connections with big-city politics. The event was hearings by the Senate Special Committee to Investigate Organized Crime, popularly called the Kefauver Committee after its chairman, Senator Estes Kefauver of Tennessee.

The committee had begun hearings in May 1950 in various cities. Local TV stations presented the hearings as a routine public service, and the broadcasts didn't create a stir.

Then the hearings came to the capital of the communications industry, New York, which had facilities for network transmission and which had increased its area audience in the previous twelve months from 29 to 51 percent. Suddenly, 30 million households in twenty cities were watching the hearings live.

Here was a new national experience, right in the living room. It was not to be missed, an inside look at big-city corruption. On one side, there were the committee's five U.S. senators—dignified, judicial, projecting an air of authority. Their brilliant chief counsel, Rudolph Halley, did most of the tough questioning for them. On the other side, there were sinister underworld figures and crooked politicians being called to account.

The televised hearings resembled a shoot-out in a Western movie, with Halley playing the role of law-and-order sheriff. He fired off the questions. The witnesses tried to shoot back, but their answers were evasive, embarrassing, and often incriminating.

Kefauver's biographer, Joseph Bruce Gorman,

called the confrontations "a human drama so exciting and full of suspense that had it been submitted as fiction it would have been rejected as unrealistic."

Even the underworld watched! *Life* ran a large photo of gambling king Joe Adonis staring intently at a sixteen-inch TV screen in his Palisade, New Jersey, living room. In a memorable exchange at the hearing, when "Greasy Thumb" Guzik refused to answer questions on the grounds that "it might incriminate me," he was asked whether he was acting on his lawyer's advice. "No," he replied, "I heard it on television."

One unforgettable image in particular epitomized the power of TV to command national attention. It was a pair of hands. That's right, *hands*.

The hands filled the screen. They poured a glass of water, drummed on the table, squeezed a handkerchief. The hands sweated and shook, tore pieces of paper into shreds, clenched into fists. They never rested.

And the TV audience was transfixed.

The hands belonged to the notorious Frank Costello, identified as the leader of organized crime in New York with connections that crisscrossed the country.

On March 13, 1951, millions watched as Costello's lawyer objected to TV cameras in the hearing room. The Senate committee agreed not to televise Costello's face but accepted a technician's suggestion to show only Costello's hands. Back and forth, question and answer, the audience heard Costello's gravelly voice dodge Halley's questions—and watched his twitching hands.

Costello was called back two days later. This time, he suddenly refused to answer any more questions. "I am going to walk out," he said.

And he did, with 30 million Americans watching. His refusal led to an eighteen-month sentence in Lewisburg Federal Penitentiary for contempt of Congress.

Costello was one of fifty witnesses during the eight days of the New York hearings, each adding to the real-life drama. The audience ratings in New York City were twice as high as those for the hometown Yankees when they had won the World Series the previous September. Consolidated Edison had to add an extra generator to power all the televisions that were tuned in.

One housewife, responding to a New York reporter who phoned for her reaction to the hearings, exclaimed, "It is positively the most wonderful thing I ever saw." Then she told him not to detain her any longer—she wanted to get back to her TV set. A man in Philadelphia was so engrossed in the TV hearings that he didn't notice that his shed was destroyed by fire. He didn't look up until the fire reached the upper story of his home.

Overnight, Kefauver was elevated from an ambitious southern senator to a national hero, his face on magazine covers, his book on crime a best-seller. When introduced at a newspaper convention, he was described as "a man who probably has been looked at by more people than any man in American history up to today."

Kefauver emerged as a leading contender for the nomination as presidential candidate of the Democratic Party in 1952. He didn't get the nomination, but his TV fame paved the way for his nomination in 1956 for vice president (running with unsuccessful presidential nominee Adlai E. Stevenson).

Halley, Kefauver's counsel, was transformed from a

novice to a power in New York City politics. As a reform candidate in the fall of 1951, he defeated both Democratic and Republican nominees to become president of the New York City Council.

TV critic Jack Gould of the *New York Times* identified what happened in the Kefauver hearings. They "demonstrated with awesome vividness what television can do to enlighten, to educate and to drive home a lesson."

For the country as a whole, the Kefauver hearings increased awareness of political corruption and aroused public indignation against organized crime. The hearings didn't eliminate organized crime, but they did affect popular attitudes. Underworld kingpins lost their romantic aura; reformers won renown.

The hearings were the first of many televised confrontations. Time and again in the decades that followed, congressional hearings would command huge audiences.

Newspaper and news magazine coverage built interest. The stage was set, the participants took their places, and as real-life drama unfolded, TV magnified the event and focused America's attention on it. As *Life* magazine said of the Kefauver hearings, the event became "almost the sole subject of national conversation."

3
1950s POLITICS:

THE " SPECTACULAR " INFLUENCE OF TV

THE CHECKERS SPEECH

When Richard M. Nixon walked into a hotel coffee shop on the morning of September 24, 1952, the waitresses couldn't believe their eyes. They almost fainted—not because he was the Republican candidate for vice president, but because they had seen him on television the evening before in a dramatic thirty-minute appearance.

Before an audience of 60 million, Nixon established television as the most powerful weapon in U.S. politics. His landmark broadcast was called the Checkers speech after the Nixon family dog that provided the emotional high point of his address.

Nixon turned to television because he was in imminent danger of being dropped as Dwight D. Eisenhower's running mate after a *New York Post* report on the "millionaire's club." The *Post*'s banner headline thundered:

SECRET RICH MEN'S TRUST FUND KEEPS
NIXON IN STYLE BEYOND HIS SALARY

Closeups taken from a TV screen at NBC, New York, of Richard M. Nixon delivering the Checkers speech, September 23, 1952. (AP/Wide World Photos)

Actually, the Nixon fund, which amounted to only $18,235, was not illegal. But the highly publicized story left a strong impression of scandal, which was at odds with Eisenhower's determination to run a presidential campaign as "clean as a hound's tooth." The Republican leadership was ready to dump Nixon in the face of the bad publicity. They didn't want to lose the election because of him.

Nixon decided to use television to go over the heads of professional politicians and speak face-to-face with American voters. Half of the TV sets in the country were tuned in as he sat at a desk in a plain studio of El Capitan Theater in Hollywood. His wife, Pat, sat nearby in an armchair, listening.

Nixon confronted the charges head-on. He explained that the fund, which was legal, dated from his successful 1950 California campaign for the U.S. Senate and was used strictly for campaign purposes.

He told the TV audience that he was going to do something "unprecedented in the history of American politics" in order to show that he had not "feathered" his own nest. He gave "a complete financial history, everything I have earned, everything I have spent, everything I own." He owned a two-year-old Oldsmobile and owed ten thousand dollars on his California house and twenty thousand dollars on his Washington house.

Nixon laid it all out before the American people in a folksy, I'm-just-like-you style, presenting himself as "a man of modest means." He had the audience in the palm of his hand when he talked about his wife. Pat "doesn't have a mink coat," he said. She has a "perfectly respectable Republican cloth coat."

Then he recalled the day he picked up a gift for his two children after winning the nomination for vice president. It was unforgettable television.

"You know what it [the gift] was?" Nixon asked.

"It was a little cocker spaniel in a crate . . . sent all the way from Texas—black and white, spotted, and our little girl Tricia, the six-year-old, named it Checkers. And you know, the kids, like all kids, love that dog, and I just want to say this, right now, that regardless of what they say about it, we're going to keep it."

Nixon closed with an appeal to his listeners to write and wire the Republican National Committee whether or not he should remain on the Eisenhower ticket.

After the speech, Nixon was in tears. He was sure that it was an "utter flop" and upset that he had lost track of the time and hadn't included the address of the Republican National Committee so Americans could "write and wire."

He couldn't have been more wrong. He underrated the impact of an emotional heart-to-heart talk on the American public. He underestimated the power of TV. Nixon succeeded much more than he or anyone else had expected. Eisenhower watched and was impressed. Even the hardened studio cameramen had tears in their eyes. His hotel lobby burst into cheers when he returned after his speech.

Most important, Nixon won direct, overpowering public support. More than a million people sent letters and telegrams backing him. He had hit a very responsive chord among Americans with the right touch of sentimentality. He didn't sound high and mighty. He sounded like one of them.

Thanks to the speech, Nixon overcame the doubts

of Republican Party leaders. He kept his place as vice presidential nominee and was elected along with Eisenhower.

Checkers became the most famous pet in the country and was flooded with gifts: dog collars, blankets, a year's supply of dog food.

Nixon biographer Garry Wills summed up the speech's significance: "That broadcast saved Nixon's career, and made history."

In his memoirs, Nixon agreed: "If it hadn't been for that broadcast, I would never have been around to run for the Presidency."

Theodore H. White, the celebrated author of the *Making of the President* books, wrote that Nixon had discovered "how spectacular the influence of television could be." It enabled him to go directly to the people, to stir their emotions, and to override the power of the party leaders.

"Television," White predicted, "would change the mechanics of all future American campaigning."

And it has.

4

1950s WAR:

" THE SIDE OF WAR
WE DON'T SEE VERY MUCH OF "

THE KOREAN WAR

General William Tecumseh Sherman, the U.S. Civil War general known for his destructive march through rebellious Georgia and South Carolina, looked back in disgust at war with a memorable comment: "War is at best barbarism. I am tired and sick of war. Its glory is all moonshine. It is only those who have neither fired a shot nor heard the shrieks and groans of the wounded who cry aloud for blood, more vengeance, more desolation. War is hell."

Seventy-one years after Sherman made that comment, television began demonstrating how it can bring home the experience of war as "hell" and can do so while war is still raging. The setting was the mountainous six-hundred-mile-long Korean peninsula.

War broke out at 4:00 A.M. Korean time, on Saturday, June 24, 1950, at the 38th parallel, the dividing line between North Korea and South Korea. Communist North Korea "struck like a cobra," U.S. General Douglas MacArthur said of the surprise invasion.

See It Now camera crew filming members of the 25th U.S. Infantry Division on location in Korea, December 1, 1953. (U.S. Army photo by Corporal Flinn (6BC), 25th Signal Corps, National Archives)

The attack was a direct challenge to the United Nations (UN). With the defeat of Japan in World War II, Korea had been freed from Japanese colonial rule and granted independence as a United Nations ward. North Korea (the Democratic People's Republic) came under Communist rule, while South Korea (the Republic of Korea) was under UN protection.

On the Tuesday evening after the invasion, the UN Security Council voted to use force against the aggressor. It was the first time an international organization had done that. Another UN resolution, this one on July 7, stipulated that all military forces contributed by UN members be under U.S. command. President Truman turned that command over to General MacArthur, a World War II hero in the victory over Japan, and committed air, ground, and sea forces to what became an "undeclared war."

Americans turned to radio for the latest news and to newspapers for detailed reports. Without benefit of communications satellites, TV couldn't keep up with the other media in fast delivery of news.

But TV was unsurpassed in depicting what war was like, particularly in documentaries. It showed what war did to those who fought and how men and women faced its danger, destruction, and death. It showed the boredom and the fear of men preparing for battle and the agony of the wounded after a battle. It also showed what happened to innocent victims.

In one memorable TV report, Bill Downs of CBS described the devastation in a war-ravaged village. All around him, houses were reduced to rubble, poor farmers in shock. Downs couldn't control his reaction. He wept. Then the camera captured the essence of the report in a single image: a forlorn old man walking down what had once been a street, holding a child's hand. "This," reported Downs, "is the side of war we don't see very much of, but probably it's the most important part of all."

The seesaw war lasted three years, one month, and two days. At the start, the North Koreans quickly captured the South Korean capital of Seoul and threatened to drive UN forces off the Korean peninsula.

But MacArthur saved the day with a bold end run. He directed an assault from the sea at the port city of Inchon, twenty-four miles west of Seoul. He not only liberated Seoul, he had the entire North Korean army on the run. UN forces were back in control of South Korea.

MacArthur didn't stop there. He was determined to liberate all Korea right up to China's border. He ignored Communist China's warning that it would enter the war if he crossed the 38th parallel, which divided South Korea from North Korea. China responded by sending 300,000 troops into North Korea to drive UN forces back into South Korea.

The Communists took Seoul a second time, and only after what historian William Manchester described as "grim, colorless, and depressing" fighting, did the UN forces regain Seoul.

One year after the 1950 invasion, both sides were back where they had started: at the 38th parallel. They agreed to negotiate. But it took two years of frustrating talks and more dead and wounded before the Korean War ended on July 27, 1953. The toll was about three million dead (80 percent of them civilians), fifty-four thousand of them Americans.

In Korea, television began learning how to cover a war. It was tough going. Correspondents worked with equipment that was hard to carry into the field and limited in versatility. The film was black and white and often without sound. Film footage traveled by propeller planes and took from three days to a week to reach headquarters in New York City.

Two landmark broadcasts in the CBS *See It Now* documentary series showed TV at its best. The first, at Christmastime 1951, showed soldiers at war—moving equipment, slogging through the mud, bantering back and forth against a backdrop of destruction and death. The program ended with soldiers identifying themselves and their hometowns on camera.

Famed journalist Edward R. Murrow, who produced and narrated the series, concluded the show by announcing that in the short time since the scenes were shot, half of the soldiers just seen had been wounded, killed, or reported missing in action!

The show earned a critic's praise that it was "the first Korea report that actually brought the war home to us."

In 1952, *See It Now* presented "Christmas in Korea." Once again, the story of war was told in terms of the people fighting it—soldiers on the front lines, pilots at their combat stations, the wounded in the hospital. Each told viewers how he felt, and then Murrow ended by saying: "There is no conclusion to this report from Korea because there is no end to the war."

Reactions were emotional and enthusiastic. TV critics spoke for the audience. Ben Gross of the *New York Daily News* said the documentary provided "the most graphic and yet sensitive pictures of war we have ever seen." John Crosby of the *New York Herald Tribune* said it captured "the humanity of an essentially inhuman profession."

From then on, as long as television was on hand, people at home would see the real face of war.

5
1950s HEROES AND VILLAINS:

" NO GREATER FEAT OF JOURNALISTIC ENTERPRISE "

JOSEPH R. McCARTHY

In the 1950s, TV focused its magnifying screen on a junior senator from Wisconsin who was described in 1953 as the second most powerful individual in the United States.

As chairman of the Senate Permanent Subcommittee on Investigations, Republican Senator Joseph R. McCarthy had the power to ruin government officials, politicians, and private citizens—anyone he accused of Communist sympathies or affiliations. His accusations alone, without supporting evidence, were enough to destroy careers and undermine lives. He openly said: "I don't answer charges, I make them."

He capitalized on widespread fear of communism. America's cold war against the Soviet Union was beginning to heat up. Politicians and the press created an atmosphere of suspicion: The Soviets were out to get us! McCarthy fed the fear and spread the suspicion, but he never exposed a single Communist spy.

No one was safe from his charges—high-ranking

Washington *Star* promotional photograph of Senator Joseph R. McCarthy wielding a "new broom" on the Capitol steps c. 1954. (Copyright © The *Washington Post*. Reprinted by permission of the D.C. Public Library)

government officials, diplomats, professors, dentists, actors, scientists—even the U.S. Army.

McCarthy's witch hunt made its way into the language. *Webster's New World Dictionary* defines McCarthyism as "the use of indiscriminate, often unfounded, accusations, sensationalism, inquisitorial investigative methods, etc., ostensibly in the suppression of communism."

McCarthyism was born on Thursday, February 9, 1950, in Wheeling, West Virginia. Senator McCarthy attracted nationwide publicity by delivering a speech charging that there were Communists in the U.S. State Department. From then on, he conducted what Walter Lippmann, the newspaper columnist, called a "cold, calculated, sustained and ruthless effort to make himself feared."

He succeeded. Tens of millions of Americans regarded him as the symbol of anticommunism. The Gallup Poll consistently reported that half of all Americans had a "favorable opinion" of McCarthy. Then on the evening of March 9, 1954, Edward R. Murrow, the most distinguished journalist in broadcasting, devoted his CBS *See It Now* documentary program to exploring McCarthy's methods.

In thirty minutes of prime-time TV viewed in thirty-six cities, brief film clips showed McCarthy making unfounded charges; then Murrow followed with evidence that refuted McCarthy—again and again.

The effect was devastating: the documentary showed McCarthy belching, laughing at his own vulgar jokes, abusing witnesses, contradicting himself. When the facts followed McCarthy's statements, his own words were turned against him.

Murrow concluded by warning that McCarthyism

was a dangerous weapon to use in fighting communism. The camera zeroed in on Murrow. His furrowed brow and piercing eyes filled the screen. His dramatic voice measured every word as he challenged Americans to face up to McCarthyism:

> *We proclaim ourselves, as indeed we are, the defenders of freedom—what's left of it— but we cannot defend freedom abroad by deserting it at home. The actions of the junior senator from Wisconsin have caused alarm and dismay amongst our allies abroad and given considerable comfort to our enemies. And whose fault is that? Not really his. He didn't create this situation of fear, he merely exploited it; and rather successfully. Cassius was right: "The fault, dear Brutus, is not in our stars but in ourselves."*

CBS received more than a hundred thousand letters, telegrams, and telephone calls praising Murrow. His supporters included former President Harry S. Truman, Chief Justice Earl Warren of the U.S. Supreme Court, and the celebrated Nobel Prize physicist Albert Einstein.

Broadcasting and Telecasting magazine said that "no greater feat of journalistic enterprise has occurred in modern times." In his history of broadcast journalism, Edward Bliss Jr. singled out Murrow's concluding statement as "probably the most forceful editorial ever delivered on radio or television."

Two days after the Murrow broadcast, television turned its cameras on a public hearing of the Senate's

Permanent Subcommittee on Investigations. McCarthy was using the hearing to bully witnesses and make headlines. He accused a witness named Annie Lee Moss, a civilian U.S. Army clerk, of being a Communist with access to army secrets. But the frail, soft-spoken African-American widow in her late forties quickly won over the committee with her obvious innocence. She knew nothing about communism; as for access to army secrets, she had never been in a code room in her life. A less likely spy couldn't be found in all Washington. When Senator Stuart Symington, a subcommittee member, said before the cameras that he was convinced that Mrs. Moss was "telling the truth," the audience at the hearing applauded and cheered. He won more applause when he denounced the vicious methods of McCarthy and the subcommittee's twenty-six-year-old chief counsel, Roy Cohn.

The emotional climax came when Symington turned to Mrs. Moss, who had been fired from her army job, and told her that if the army didn't take her back (it did), he personally would get her a job.

When McCarthy's charges boomeranged, he abruptly left the hearing room, claiming he had "an important appointment." The TV cameras focused on his empty chair.

The Moss hearing was an "unmitigated disaster for McCarthy and Cohn," noted McCarthy biographer Thomas C. Reeves. Its impact was heightened when Murrow devoted a second *See It Now* show to the Moss hearing, a week after the first McCarthy program.

When CBS gave McCarthy airtime to reply, he called Murrow a "leader of the jackal pack which is always found at the throat of anyone who dares to expose Communists and traitors." CBS, in turn, issued a statement affirming their confidence in Murrow.

The Moss episode was only a warm-up for what happened next. For thirty-five days beginning April 22, 1954, television covered McCarthy as he took on the entire U.S. Army. He charged that "certain individuals in the army have been promoting, covering up, and honorably discharging known Communists."

The army struck back with charges against McCarthy, Chief Counsel Roy Cohn, and G. David Schine, a multimillionaire playboy who had been on the subcommittee staff until he was drafted. The army charged that Cohn went all out to get special treatment for Private Schine with warnings of investigations and political reprisals, and that he had even threatened to "wreck the army."

As the *New York Times* reported in a giant front-page headline:

ARMY CHARGES MCCARTHY AND COHN THREATENED IT IN TRYING TO OBTAIN PREFERRED TREATMENT FOR SCHINE.

Viewers rushed to watch televised hearings on the charges, since McCarthy was by then "a national obsession," as columnist Walter Lippmann noted. Soap-opera addicts deserted their favorite programs on CBS and NBC to watch the hearings on ABC. At one point, nine out of ten Americans interviewed by the Gallup Poll said they had followed the hearings on TV. What they saw, as one study pointed out, "was a calamity" for McCarthy.

He couldn't chair the proceedings since they were investigating charges against him, but this didn't prevent McCarthy from displaying his bullying, high-handed tactics. In a whining, insinuating monotone, he kept interrupting the proceedings by exclaiming "point of order."

These interruptions turned the audience against him. He even became the butt of editorial cartoons and jokes. TV comedians mimicked him on the air by shouting, "Mr. Chairman, Mr. Chairman," and "Point of order."

Ultimately, McCarthy was vanquished by an unlikely opponent: a tall, birdlike lawyer from Boston named Joseph N. Welch, who wore green bow ties and spoke in a squeaky voice. Welch questioned McCarthy as legal counsel for the U.S. Army.

Welch upstaged McCarthy and put him on the defensive, a new experience for McCarthy. Before a hushed audience at the hearing, a frustrated McCarthy tried to strike back by charging that a member of Welch's law firm had belonged to a Communist organization. In 1954, that kind of accusation was enough to ruin anyone's career.

The TV audience watched McCarthy snicker and then watched Welch deliver an eloquent defense of his young colleague. He had, indeed, joined a controversial lawyers' group while in law school, but resigned a few months after graduation. As Welch made clear, that was no reason to smear a young lawyer who in no way could be considered a Communist or Communist sympathizer.

"Until this moment, Senator, I think I never really gauged your cruelty or your recklessness," Welch said.

His knockout punch was delivered in words that became better known than any advertising slogan:

"Have you no sense of decency, sir, at long last? Have you no sense of decency?"

The audience at the hearing cheered. McCarthy was stunned. Even his allies realized that he had gone too far. Newspapers ran the headline, HAVE YOU NO SENSE OF DECENCY? For weeks, TV reran the McCarthy-Welch clash. Although the committee dismissed the charges, cheers for McCarthy changed to jeers, and Welch became a national hero.

Whereas Murrow had showed how McCarthy was an opportunist who made irresponsible accusations, the army hearings drove the message home. On December 2, 1954, by a vote of sixty-seven to twenty-two, the Senate condemned McCarthy. The resolution stated that his conduct was "contrary to senatorial traditions and is hereby condemned."

Although he remained a senator until 1957, McCarthy had lost his power. TV stopped focusing its cameras on him, and the nation stopped paying attention.

6

1950s EYE-OPENERS:

" WAITING OUTSIDE THE AMERICAN HOME... WAS A HUMAN FACE THAT HAD SELDOM ENTERED THERE "

THE INTEGRATION OF
LITTLE ROCK CENTRAL HIGH SCHOOL

On the first day of school in Little Rock, Arkansas, in 1957, fifteen-year-old Elizabeth Eckford got up early, pressed the new black-and-white dress she had made for the occasion, and ate breakfast with her parents. She had transferred to a new school, Little Rock Central High, because it offered a speech course that could help prepare her to be a lawyer someday.

On arriving at school, Elizabeth walked toward the entrance where National Guard troopers stood with bayonets on their rifles. They let other students in but blocked her way. The other students were white, Elizabeth was black.

All around, an angry white mob closed in on her. Someone screamed, "Lynch her! Lynch her!"

John Chancellor, who later became a famous NBC news anchor, was at the scene, "terribly frightened for her, frightened for himself, frightened about what this told him about his country" (as recounted by author David Halberstam).

Elizabeth Eckford—one of nine black students admitted to Little Rock Central High School by federal court order—braving a jeering crowd on the first day of school, September 4, 1957. (UPI/Bettmann)

Here was a solitary schoolgirl, calm and dignified, threatened by a flood of rage and fury. All she wanted to do was go to school. All that concerned the mob was the color of her skin. For Chancellor, this was the ugliest mob he had ever encountered.

With the help of an elderly white woman, Elizabeth escaped to a bus stop and managed to board a bus and get away. For her, it was a terrifying experience; for many in the network audience it was eye-opening. Network TV cameras showed racism up close.

Between September 2 and 27, 1957, TV journalism began to come of age. The Little Rock story became the "first running story of national importance that television fully covered," as a *New York Times* commentary noted.

TV demonstrated that it could bring home the power, fury, and emotion of a major controversy in a way the printed word could never match. In this instance, as in others to come, many Americans would have preferred to evade the issue. And they could have if it weren't for television.

At that point, it had been three years since the U.S. Supreme Court declared racial segregation in public schools unconstitutional and ordered desegregation to proceed "with all deliberate speed." When school opened on September 4, 1957, Little Rock Central High was planning to comply.

It was a modest beginning. Nine African-American children had been selected to join two thousand white children on opening day. The local police and the mayor expected everything to go smoothly—until the governor of Arkansas, Orval E. Faubus, decided to defy the U.S. Constitution and stir up trouble.

Faubus was in danger of losing his campaign for re-election and saw a chance to win the votes of opponents of integration. He called out the National Guard to stop the nine children from registering for school. He claimed he did it to keep the peace, but he knew otherwise. He was playing dirty politics. As an extensive FBI investigation confirmed, racial conflict was not a serious threat in Little Rock.

Faubus's actions attracted segregationists from all over the state. A police official reported that "half the troublemakers were from out of town." Little Rock's mayor complained of "professional agitators." They brought mob rule to Central High.

Faubus was forced by a federal court order to let the African-American students into school, but the situation only became worse. The local police had taken over from the Arkansas militia and confronted a white mob that grew larger and more menacing each day. The police could not control it. The black children had to be withdrawn from school.

President Eisenhower had no choice but to enforce the federal law. Otherwise, as he told the nationwide TV audience, "anarchy would result."

Crack troops of the 101st Airborne Division dispersed the wild-eyed protesters by pointing bayonets at their throats. Platoons of paratroopers formed a semi-circle of protection around the nine determined African-American children, and running at the double, escorted them into Little Rock Central High School to stay.

For many white southerners, the episode was a shocking replay of their ancestors' defeat in the U.S. Civil War and humiliation in the subsequent Reconstruction. TV coverage inflamed their outrage at the arrival of northern soldiers on southern soil. The Gallup Poll found that two-thirds of southerners opposed the intervention of federal troops compared with only 10 percent of Americans in northern and western states.

Faubus, as he had hoped, won a massive victory in his campaign for reelection and remained governor of Arkansas until he retired in 1967. He became a hero throughout many parts of the South.

But the younger generation of southern blacks had seen that racism could be successfully challenged. Historian William Manchester pointed out that Little Rock left a "profound impression" on African Americans. They realized that they could stand up for their rights.

TV had unmasked the face of racism for white America. All over the country, people recognized the face as their own.

Wallace Westfeldt, who covered civil rights in the 1950s as a newspaper reporter and later produced the NBC nightly news, testified to the difference TV had made: "Even without any commentary, a shot of a big white man spitting and cursing at black children did more to open up the national intellect than my [newspaper] stories ever could."

Robert Kintner, who was president of NBC, pinpointed the significance of the Little Rock coverage: "Waiting outside the American home, in the days before television, was a human face that seldom had entered there: the Negro citizen, who was not welcome as a guest, a colleague, an acquaintance. Television put Negro Americans into the living rooms of tens of millions of white Americans for the first time."

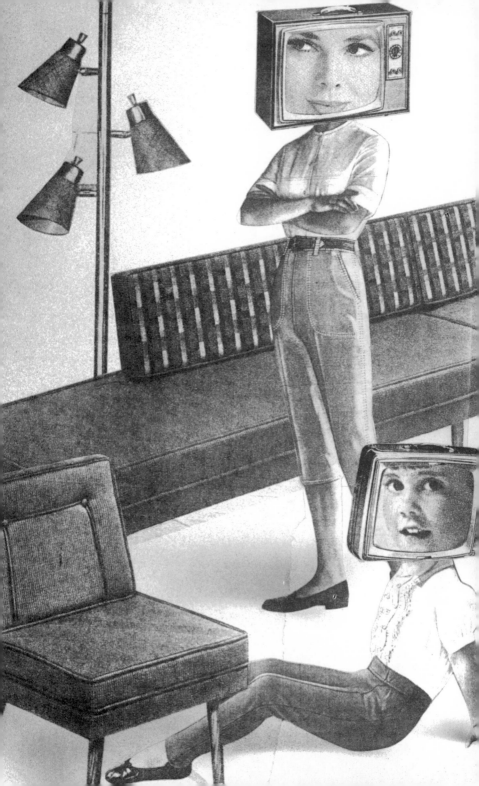

7

THE 1960s:

" BUT WE NEVER GOT A CHANCE TO STOP "

The decade of the 1960s was a time of rebellion. A noisy generation replaced the Silent Generation of the 1950s, its voice heard loudly on the streets and campuses of the United States—and on television.

Belief in "our country, right or wrong" was replaced by "Hell No, We Won't Go" as young Americans resisted being drafted for the Vietnam War.

Music became loud and hair long. Young Americans listened devotedly to the Beatles. Rock 'n' roll was here to stay. Songs and music of protest separated children from their parents. Banners and buttons proclaimed: "Don't trust anyone over thirty!"

Historian Garry Wills looked back at the 1960s and concluded: "It is hard to exaggerate the disorienting pace of change in that period." When Americans turned on the television set, they didn't know if they would be shocked, amazed, repelled, outraged, saddened, or uplifted. Something was always happening.

"But we never got a chance to stop," *Newsweek* stated in summarizing the decade. "No time-outs, no rest periods, not even any sidelines—those seemed to be the rules of the game during the frantic '60s."

TV was in 95 percent of U.S. households by 1965. The 515 TV stations in 1960 increased to 569 in 1965 and 677 in 1970. In 1963, polls reported that television had passed newspapers as the country's leading source of news.

Nineteen sixty-three was also the year (on Labor Day) that CBS introduced the half-hour evening network news. So did NBC. ABC followed in 1967. From 1965 onward, the news was broadcast in living color.

Chet and David at NBC (Chet Huntley and David Brinkley) were the first superstar nightly news anchors. Their sign-off became household words: "Good night, Chet. . . . Good night, David." Such was the power of the nightly news that Senator Robert F. Kennedy said in 1966 that he would rather have "30 seconds on an evening news program than coverage in every newspaper in the world."

A full-scale study of TV anchors by Barbara Matusow concluded: "Uninvited, unelected, and with almost no public debate, they [TV anchors] have taken their place beside presidents, congressmen, labor leaders, industrialists, and others who shape public policy and private attitudes."

TV anchors became guides leading Americans from one landmark event to another. Faithful audiences took it for granted that the anchors would tell them what it all meant.

TV journalism went further in the 1960s by producing stunning documentaries. Producers identified a topic, problem, or situation that cried out for attention, then went out with cameras and reporters and took months, if necessary, to cover the story in depth. Titles ranged from "Hunger in America" to the "Biography of a Bookie Joint." Perhaps the most ambitious was a four-hour, prime-time ABC documentary on Africa. It brought America a whole new understanding of cultures and countries they knew practically nothing about.

As producer Don Hewitt, a master of the documentary medium, pointed out: "People identify with people. Television is best, not when imparting information, but when you let people share in an experience."

That's what happened during the 1960s, a decade in which TV news and documentaries brought the nation together in shared experiences. Repeatedly, Americans felt as did TV critic Dean Gysel of the *Chicago Daily News* when he said: "I wished I could have turned off the world by turning off the television."

Americans watched the triumph and the tragedy of John F. Kennedy.

They watched the painful accounts of assassinations of national leaders.

They watched African Americans struggle for their civil rights in bloody confrontations.

They watched the horrors of war in Vietnam.

They watched what was once a comic-strip fantasy, Americans walking on the moon.

Events that happened in the 1960s radically changed the country, with aftershocks felt to the end of the century. And these events were molded and magnified by how they were televised.

59

8

1960s CONFRONTATION:

" A GIANT BEAST...WAS DYING "

THE CIVIL RIGHTS MOVEMENT

In Oxford, Mississippi, and in Birmingham and Selma, Alabama, network television turned local civil rights confrontations into national events. Their sound and fury rumbled through the stormy 1960s, shaking millions of viewers and forcing them to confront an issue the nation had been evading since the Civil War: equality for African Americans.

TV placed civil rights at the top of the national agenda. It showed what African Americans were up against and handed their leaders a weapon of unequaled power in a democracy—the power to command national attention, to arouse the public, and to trigger government action.

In 1961, a nine-year veteran of the U.S. Air Force, James H. Meredith, applied to the all-white University of Mississippi. On his application, he identified himself as "an American-Mississippi-Negro citizen."

Ole Miss, as the school was known in the South, rejected his application, supposedly on academic grounds. Meredith sued, charging that race was the real

The Reverend Martin Luther King Jr. (front row, left) leading the March on Washington for Jobs and Freedom, August 28, 1963. (National Archives)

reason. Meredith's case was fought all the way up to the U.S. Supreme Court, which in September 1962 ordered Ole Miss to enroll Meredith.

"Never!" Mississippi Governor Ross Barnett responded, setting the stage for bloody confrontations.

On September 20, 1962, Barnett personally turned Meredith away when he tried to register. Hostile crowds gathered at the Ole Miss campus in Oxford, Mississippi. The Federal Bureau of Investigation (FBI) received reports that vigilantes had come from distant states with rifles and beer coolers, swearing to "defend" Mississippi.

The climax was reached during the evening of Sunday, September 30, after 123 deputy federal marshals, 316 U.S. border patrolmen, and 97 federal prison guards escorted Meredith onto campus. The mob, exceeding 2,000, went wild. More than 300 people were injured. Two people were killed, including a French journalist.

By the next morning, federal troops had to intervene. They forced the raging mob to retreat and cleared the way for Meredith to register. By transferring two years of college credit, he entered as a junior (eventually graduating in 1963).

Meredith's lawyer, Constance Baker Motley, saw Mississippi's resistance as "playing out the last chapter of the Civil War." The ferocity of racism was portrayed night after night in the evening news and a half-dozen network documentaries.

The year that followed, 1963, was a year of great anger and rage: righteous anger of African Americans impatient about progress toward equality; bitter rage among segregationists and racists opposed to it. There were more than nine hundred demonstrations in more than a hundred cities, more than twenty thousand people arrested, and at least ten related deaths.

The spotlight shifted to Birmingham, Alabama, which civil rights leader Martin Luther King Jr. called "the most segregated" city in the United States. Its police commissioner, Eugene "Bull" Connor, took stubborn pride in keeping Birmingham that way.

Blacks and whites had separate—but not equal—public toilets, drinking fountains, parks, playgrounds, restaurants, schools, and churches. The violence necessary to back up segregation earned the city the menacing nickname "Bombingham." In early April 1963, King and his followers came to organize sit-ins and marches to demand an end to segregation. Connor was true to character. He arrested more than four hundred protesters the first day and continued to make arrests until the jails overflowed.

On May 2, more than one thousand African-American children gathered in a Baptist church and began a march for freedom singing the anthem of the civil rights movement, "We Shall Overcome." They were promptly arrested on Bull Connor's orders.

The next day more children marched, and in the turmoil that followed, Connor ordered firemen to turn high-pressure hoses and police dogs on them. The nation watched the TV coverage, horrified.

Connor's tactics boomeranged. The images of police attacking helpless children did more for promoting civil rights than any protester could have hoped. David Vann, a white lawyer working to reform Birmingham, described the power of the images: "[W]hen the police dogs arrived and they started the hoses, the water, that

just created very dramatic pictures. There was no way Dr. King could have bought that kind of thing. The ball game was all over, once the hoses and the dogs were brought on."

Confronted with the nationally televised brutality in Birmingham, President John F. Kennedy faced up to the "moral crisis" in the country and ordered his aides to prepare a major antisegregation bill.

In June 1963, Kennedy reminded a national TV audience of what was at stake: "[T]his nation . . . will not be fully free until all its citizens are free. . . . It is time to act in the Congress, in your state . . . above all, in all our daily lives."

On August 28, 1963, more than a quarter million people gathered in Washington, D.C., for the March on Washington for Jobs and Freedom in support of the civil rights movement. The incredible scene was captured by a CBS TV camera mounted at the top of the Washington Monument: an ocean of people on both sides of the reflecting pool and all around the base of the Lincoln Memorial.

Millions of television viewers, including President Kennedy, heard a complete Martin Luther King Jr. speech for the first time. They heard King's historic description of his hope for America:

> I have a dream that one day this nation will rise up and live out the true meaning of its creed: "We hold these truths to be self-evident; that all men are created equal."
>
> I have a dream that one day on the red hills of Georgia sons of former slaves and the sons of former slaveowners will be able to sit

down together at the table of brotherhood.

I have a dream that one day even the state of Mississippi, a desert state sweltering with the heat of injustice and oppression, will be transformed into an oasis of freedom and justice.

I have a dream that my four little children will one day live in a nation where they will not be judged by the color of their skin but by the content of their character.

The networks covered the speech live and also featured it in special evening reports. On Labor Day, following the march, NBC devoted its entire nighttime schedule to a three-hour documentary entitled, "The American Revolution of '63." Thanks to the television coverage, an increasing number of white Americans were supporting King's dream and demanding government action to bring it about.

But the battle had only begun, as *Time* magazine reminded its readers almost two years later: "Despite great gains in the past decade, the American Negro is still often denied the most basic right of citizenship under constitutional government—the right to vote."

The comment was prompted by another march, this one on Selma, Alabama, where more than 50 percent of the population was African American, but only 1 percent of eligible blacks were registered to vote. For seven weeks in early 1965, King led marches to the county courthouse in Selma seeking to register African-American voters.

Once again, there was a made-for-television villain who became the focus of attention: a short-tempered, segregationist police official, Sheriff Jim Clark. He wore a button on his shirt that echoed Governor Barnett at Ole Miss: *Never!*

Clark's police officers, armed with cattle prods, roughed up marching men, women, and children, arresting two thousand of them. The TV cameras captured the unrestrained behavior of the police in graphic detail.

In nearby Marion, fifty state troopers and a band of vigilantes attacked four hundred African-American demonstrators. A young woodcutter among the protestors, Jimmie Lee Jackson, was shot in the stomach. Before he died eight days later, he reported that a state trooper had gunned him down. Jackson's murder heightened the tension.

Richard Valeriani of NBC was covering the Marion demonstration when he was struck with an ax handle and had to be hospitalized. A state trooper standing nearby just took away the ax handle and said matter-of-factly to the attacker: "I guess you've done enough damage with that tonight." The next day Valeriani broadcast from his hospital bed, his head bandaged, his speech slurred, but his message clear about terror in Alabama.

Next, local civil rights leaders announced a protest march from Selma to the Alabama state capital of Montgomery on Sunday, March 7, 1965. About 650 African-American marchers and some white supporters defied a ban by Alabama Governor George C. Wallace and headed out of Selma via the Pettus Bridge.

Clark and his forces were waiting. He gave a two-minute warning, and then deputies on horseback and state troopers wearing gas masks attacked. The mounted deputies rode into the marchers wielding billy clubs and wet bullwhips. The troopers let loose tear gas. No one was safe. Bystanders as well as marchers were chased and beaten. Men, women, and children were screaming, running, bleeding, knocked to the ground, clubbed as rampaging deputies and troopers scattered the marchers.

ABC interrupted a movie to air a special report about the confrontation, which dominated the evening news on all three networks. Americans all over the country responded. Thousands of them sent telegrams, signed petitions, and joined demonstrations. Popular support grew for voting rights reform.

President Lyndon Johnson rose to the occasion. He went before a rare nighttime joint session of Congress on March 15, 1965, to present a sweeping voting rights bill. His opening words set the tone: "I speak tonight for the dignity of man and the destiny of democracy." The televised forty-five-minute speech was interrupted forty times by applause, twice by standing ovations. "There is no constitutional issue here," President Johnson said.

> The command of the Constitution is plain. There is no moral issue. It is wrong . . . to deny any of your fellow Americans the right to vote. There is no issue of states' rights or national rights. There is only the struggle for human rights. . . . And should we defeat every enemy, and should we double our wealth and conquer the stars, and still be un-equal on this issue, then we will have failed as a people and a nation. . . .
> The real hero of this struggle is the Amer-

ican Negro. His actions and protests, his courage to risk safety and even . . . his life have awakened the conscience of this nation. His demonstrations have been designed to call attention to injustice. . . . And who among us can say that we would have made the same progress were it not for his persistent bravery and his faith in American democracy?

Martin Luther King Jr. watched on TV along with millions of other viewers. When the president, a man of the South, closed his speech by repeating the anthem of the civil rights movement—"We Shall Overcome"— King listened silently in his chair. And a tear ran down his cheek.

The Voting Rights Act of 1965 was passed by Congress and became law in August 1965; it is regarded as one of Johnson's greatest achievements. "Television made it possible," recalled Burke Marshall, who was at the U.S. Department of Justice when the bill passed.

Meanwhile, a new Selma-to-Montgomery march began on Sunday, March 21, after a favorable ruling by Federal Judge Frank M. Johnson Jr. that it was "constitutionally allowed." The 3,200 marchers started out on the fifty-four-mile journey under the protection of federal troops. The memorable front line of marchers was handpicked for the TV cameras: Martin Luther King Jr., Ralph Bunche (a celebrated African-American diplomat and recipient of the Nobel Peace Prize), a sharecropper in overalls, a woman college student, a rabbi, a priest, a nun, and a one-legged marcher on crutches.

When the marchers arrived in Montgomery four days later (led by the one-legged man, two flagbearers, and a piper playing "Yankee Doodle" on a fife), their numbers had swelled to twenty-five thousand. They marched to the Alabama state capitol building and sang "We Shall Overcome."

All three TV networks carried King's speech climaxing the demonstration. "Today," he cried out, "I want to say to the people of America and the nations of the world: We are not about to turn around. We are on the *move* now. Yes, we are on the move and no wave of racism can stop us. . . . We are on the move now . . . [and] not even the marching of mighty armies can halt us."

Coretta Scott King called the march into Montgomery "a great moment," coming after four "dangerous" days in which diehard segregationists threatened to kill her husband. For those four days, the networks focused national attention on the struggle for civil rights. They flew over the marchers in helicopters to film their progress and then rushed the film back in time for the evening news.

Civil rights leaders realized how much TV coverage magnified the power of their protests. "Racial prejudice had been like a giant beast that never came out in the daytime," noted the journalist-historian David Halberstam. "King and others like him were exposing it to bright light, fresh air, and the eye of the television camera, and the beast was dying."

In one troubled decade, television had done more for civil rights than had been accomplished in the almost one hundred years since the Civil War. TV not only exposed racism. It did much more. It bestowed power on those who had been powerless victims of intolerance. As long as TV watched, that tyranny became a national problem crying loudly for a solution.

9

1960s POLITICS:

" THE ATMOSPHERE OF A PRIZE FIGHT "

THE NIXON-KENNEDY PRESIDENTIAL DEBATES

A trim, tanned presidential candidate dressed smartly in dark suit, dark tie, and blue shirt stood at the podium on the left in the Chicago studio of WBBM-TV. He looked vigorous, confident, and businesslike.

His opponent at the other podium wore a light suit, pale tie, and a shirt with a collar that was too big for him. He looked tired, nervous, and in need of a shave.

Both faced the pitiless eye of TV cameras carrying the first televised presidential debate. For one hour of prime time on all three networks, 75 million Americans watched on the evening of September 26, 1960.

The candidate on the left side, Democrat John F. Kennedy, looked nothing like the underdog he was supposed to be. An unproved junior senator from Massachusetts, he faced the highly experienced Republican candidate, Richard M. Nixon.

Kennedy needed national exposure. Nixon was seasoned and already nationally known. Twice elected vice

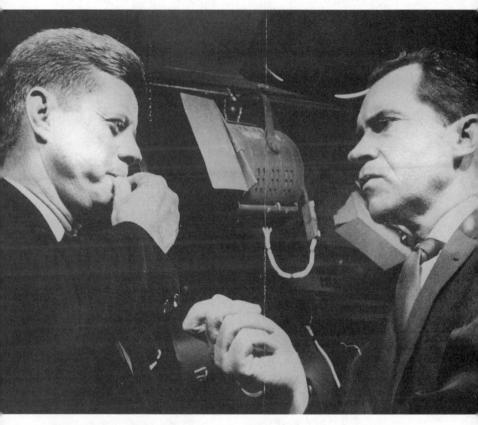

Washington *Star* photo of Senator John F. Kennedy and Vice President Richard M. Nixon taken after the second "Great Debate," October 7, 1960. (Copyright © The *Washington Post*. Reprinted by permission of the D.C. Public Library)

president, Nixon had prepared himself for eight years to take over from President Dwight D. Eisenhower.

TV critic Robert Lewis Shayon described the televised debate as if it were a boxing match: "The atmosphere was clearly that of a prize fight: the referee (producer) instructing the champ and the challenger (the candidates), the seconds (advisors) milling around, and the 'come out fighting' handshake."

The rules of the match called for an eight-minute opening statement by Kennedy followed by eight minutes from Nixon. Then a panel of four reporters would ask questions.

Kennedy won.

He won on style and image—two key ingredients for success on TV. Nixon challenged and rebutted what Kennedy said as if he were out to win debating points. He addressed Kennedy rather than the TV viewers.

On the other hand, as the celebrated chronicler of presidential campaigns Theodore H. White noted, Kennedy "was addressing himself to the audience that was the nation."

Kennedy came across as assured, energetic, dynamic. The camera was his friend.

Nixon came across as uncomfortable and ill at ease.

Nixon lost not on what he said, but on how he appeared. TV viewers saw Nixon as a gray man against the studio's gray backdrop. They saw Nixon forcing nervous smiles and perspiring under the studio lights. He "looked terrible," historian David Culbert stated.

At one point, the camera showed Nixon wiping perspiration from his brow and upper lip as he listened to Kennedy. When the camera was on Kennedy listening, he looked attentive, alert, and self-assured.

Neither candidate said anything that was memorable or headline making. The importance of style and image became obvious when audience reactions to the televised and radio versions were compared. Those who heard the debate on radio thought Nixon had won!

But what counted was the televised debate. Half the country had watched it. White had a clear verdict: "In 1960 television had won the nation away from sound to images, and that was that."

Polls showed that the crucial impact of the debates was on undecided voters. Kennedy won most of them. He came out of the televised debate feeling as well as looking like a winner. His campaign team felt a surge of optimism. In the aftermath of the TV debate, he drew larger and more excited crowds. Kennedy projected what White described as the "star quality" of television and movie idols. The Kennedy image blossomed. He was on his way to becoming America's first television president.

There were three more "Great Debates," but none had the impact and fanfare of the first. Nixon looked better and at least held his own in these three debates, but the impression created by the first one continued to cast a shadow over Nixon. Veteran Democratic politician James Farley concluded that "Nixon never got up off the floor after the first debate."

There's no way to prove the election hinged on that single hour of television. But a good case can be made for this view, given Kennedy's close margin of victory. He won by only 112,881 votes, less than two-thirds of 1 percent of the popular vote. Television was also a winner. Kennedy acknowledged its power the Monday

after his election: "It was TV more than anything else that turned the tide."

Kennedy became the first president to master the medium of television just as President Franklin D. Roosevelt had mastered radio during the 1930s and 1940s with "Fireside Chats." Images took over from words, whether spoken or written, in making the difference between political victory and defeat.

Whether in political ads, convention speeches, campaign appearances, question-and-answer programs, town meetings, talk shows, or comments before the cameras, henceforth the road to political victory became paved with TV images.

10

1960s WAR:

" LIVING-ROOM WAR "

THE VIETNAM WAR: ESCALATION

One weekend evening in 1967, as anchor Harry Reasoner finished his CBS newscast, he told his viewers that he would be away for a few weeks. He was going to Vietnam.

Before he could leave the studio, the phone rang.

A viewer was calling, Lyndon B. Johnson, the president of the United States. He wanted Reasoner to visit him at the White House before he left.

During the meeting, the president gave Reasoner, an accomplished World War II correspondent, a lecture on how to cover the war in Vietnam, on how to be a patriot, and on how to help his country.

The immediate invitation, the visit, and the lecture were a measure of how important television coverage of the Vietnam War had become to America's leaders. The nation was in the midst of the longest, most divisive, most inconclusive war in U.S. history. Television had turned it into what was labeled a "living-room war," watched nightly on the evening news.

Family watching Vietnam War coverage, February 13, 1968. (Library of Congress)

The war was taking place nine thousand miles from the White House in a Southeast Asian country of dense jungles and rice paddies. Gradually, the United States had moved from helping France, its World War II ally, to taking a pivotal role in a bloody, brutal civil war.

In the late nineteenth century, the French had invaded and taken over Indochina (now Vietnam, Cambodia, and Laos), and they were determined to hold on to it. The French benefited immensely from control of Indochina's rubber, rice, and timber exports, and they also felt a missionary zeal to "civilize" Indochina.

After World War II, the French tried for eight years—from 1946 to 1954—to crush a Vietnamese independence movement instigated by the Communist-led Vietminh. They failed. The climax came at Dien Bien Phu, where forty thousand Vietminh surrounded fifteen thousand of the best French troops, including the famous Foreign Legionnaires. The world's press focused on a fifty-six-day siege. Finally France surrendered. On May 7, 1954, the French tricolor was replaced by the Vietminh red flag with its star of gold.

The French were humiliated. "The honor of France would never be the same again," stated historian William Manchester. The Geneva Conference of 1954 instituted a cease-fire and divided Vietnam at the 17th parallel into the Communist North and the nationalist South.

The French left Vietnam, and the United States, as the world's standard-bearer against the spread of communism, was on the way in. President Eisenhower warned that if South Vietnam fell to Communist control, other Southeast Asian countries would fall, one after the other. This became known as the "domino theory."

The United States threw its money and its might behind South Vietnam to prevent a Communist takeover. With Soviet and Communist Chinese arms assistance, North Vietnam's regular army and Communist Vietcong guerrillas mounted a steady stream of military attacks. By the end of 1961, the Vietcong controlled almost half of South Vietnam.

United States involvement in South Vietnam evolved from financial support for France in 1953 to sending four hundred Special Forces advisers in 1961 to sending combat troops in 1965. Once the first troops landed on March 8, 1965, escalation was rapid. By the end of the year, 184,000 U.S. troops were in South Vietnam. Television was not far behind.

Five months after the March landing, Morley Safer of CBS News shocked America with a televised report of U.S. Marines setting fire to the Vietnamese village of Cam Ne. The marines had been sent on a search-and-destroy mission after Communist guerrillas fired on the nearby air base at Da Nang. They used matches, Zippo lighters, and flamethrowers to destroy 150 thatched huts, ignoring the pleas of old men and women to spare their homes. Three women were wounded, a ten-year-old boy was killed, and helpless villagers ran for their lives in front of the CBS cameras.

Safer's commentary challenged the Johnson administration: "To a Vietnamese peasant whose home means a lifetime of backbreaking labor, it will take more than presidential promises to convince him that we are on his side."

The televised report was totally at odds with the official image of the United States as protector of the South Vietnamese. Such TV stories fueled opposition to a war in which "it became necessary to destroy the town to save it."

President Johnson was furious about the Cam Ne report. The Pentagon wanted Safer recalled from Vietnam. Many viewers were angry at TV for covering the episode in the first place. This became a major aspect of Vietnam coverage: anger at television for what it showed and reported.

Improvements in technology made TV coverage more vivid, more immediate, and more action-packed than in the Korean War. Korean War footage took almost a week to reach New York City by propeller planes, much of it without sound. But cameramen in Vietnam mounted sound-on-film cameras on their shoulders to get close to the action. They sent the results to New York by jet, and beginning in 1967, by instant satellite transmission.

To satisfy the appetite for coverage, the number of broadcast correspondents grew rapidly after the mid-1960s. Eventually, more than two hundred correspondents, cameramen, bureau managers, producers, and sound technicians were on the scene.

In 1968, Walter Cronkite, the CBS-TV anchor voted in polls the most trusted man in the United States, came to see for himself. He couldn't have arrived at a worse time for the U.S. high command, who wanted Americans at home to believe that victory was just a matter of time.

Cronkite saw the opposite. He saw U.S. forces in South Vietnam reeling from a major enemy attack. During the Tet (Vietnamese New Year) holidays, on January 30, 1968, Vietcong guerrillas and the North Vietnamese Army launched a series of lightning attacks throughout South Vietnam. The attacks were in broad daylight in the cities, and TV cameras were on hand to contradict the military's claim that everything was under control.

Cronkite decided that he had no choice but to tell the nation the awful truth. In a half-hour prime-time news special that he wrote himself, Cronkite showed his vast and faithful TV audience what the generals and the president had failed to tell them. "Uncle Walter," as he was often called, broke the bad news to Americans who thought they couldn't lose a war. They weren't going to win in Vietnam: "It seems now more certain than ever that the bloody experience of Vietnam is to end in a stalemate. . . . To say that we are closer to victory is to believe, in the face of the evidence, the optimists who have been wrong in the past."

After watching the broadcast, President Johnson remarked to his press secretary, George Christian, that losing Cronkite's support meant that he had lost the country's support.

"Cronkite's reporting did change the balance [of opinion]," wrote David Halberstam (who won a Pulitzer Prize for his coverage of Vietnam). "It was the first time in American history a war had been declared over by an anchorman."

One month later, Johnson called for Vietnam peace talks and stunned the nation by announcing he would not seek reelection as president.

Johnson left the way open for his vice president, Hubert H. Humphrey, to win the presidential nomination at the 1968 Democratic National Convention in Chicago. Humphrey easily won on the first ballot. But outside the International Amphitheater in the streets of

Chicago the stage was set for trouble. Antiwar protesters were converging on the downtown area.

The city's iron-handed mayor, Richard J. Daley, responded by turning downtown Chicago into an armed camp. Fifty-five hundred National Guardsmen and 7,500 U.S. troops were placed on alert. To keep protesters at a distance, a seven-foot fence topped by barbed wire was set up around the convention hall. Even manhole covers in the street were sealed with tar. The situation was so touchy that the Secret Service advised President Johnson not to attend his own party's convention.

Although only ten to twelve thousand antiwar protesters actually showed up, Chicago looked and felt like a city under siege. When convention week began on Sunday, August 25, 1968, hundreds of television people were on hand with several hundred tons of equipment to cover the convention indoors and the explosive situation outside.

The climax came on Wednesday. In the afternoon, the convention had voted on a "peace plank," which condemned the United States' involvement in Vietnam. The hawks, who supported the Vietnam War, won; the doves, who opposed the war, lost. With an eye on television coverage, the antiwar demonstrators planned a protest in the evening. Despite the rejection of their request for a parade permit, they were determined to march through the streets of Chicago to the convention hall.

The police confronted the marchers at the Conrad Hilton Hotel, where the candidates were staying. The police were armed with nightsticks, guns, tear gas, and Mace, and they were backed by National Guard units.

The marchers approached the Hilton, chanting their demand: "Peace Now! Peace Now!"

Then they hailed the TV cameras: "The whole world is watching! The whole world is watching!"

Suddenly, under the glare of TV lights and cameras, the police, who had already endured days of abuse, lost control. They charged the crowd, firing tear gas, clubbing defenseless men and women, and dragging them into paddy wagons. There were screams, shouts, clouds of tear gas, and young Americans lying in the street with blood on their faces—seventeen minutes of televised mayhem.

The networks switched back and forth between the convention and the streets. Actually, NBC televised only sixty-five minutes of demonstrations (including the rioting) compared with thirty-five hours of convention proceedings; CBS thirty-two minutes compared with thirty-eight hours. A national poll reported that only 19 percent of Americans thought the police had used "too much force." To the contrary, an authoritative report by the National Commission on the Causes and Prevention of Violence concluded that the police response was "unrestrained and indiscriminate"—a "police riot." However they were perceived, those few televised minutes of violent confrontation overshadowed hours of convention coverage.

Humphrey viewed the rioting as a "catastrophe" for his election campaign. The Republican candidate, Richard M. Nixon, was reported to be "elated" as he watched on TV.

Theodore H. White wrote in his notes for one of his celebrated books on *The Making of the President*: "The Democrats are finished."

But Nixon barely won, supported by only 27 percent of the total electorate. Media historian Edward Bliss Jr. has speculated that the "ugliness accompanying his [Humphrey's] nomination, shown on television, may have elected Nixon, who squeaked to victory."

Once he was in office, it was Nixon's turn to confront the peace movement. On Saturday, November 16, 1969, more than 250,000 Americans converged on Washington, D.C., in the largest antiwar demonstration ever held in the nation's capital. Another 125,000 demonstrated in San Francisco.

Television was there as it had been throughout America's Vietnam tragedy, always delivering powerful images. Supporters and opponents of the war saw what they wanted to see in those images and TV couldn't avoid being caught in the middle.

NBC News president Reuven Frank explained why: "If we hurt them with our coverage, they say we say too much. If we hurt them by not covering, they say we say too little." Television's Vietnam chapter demonstrated the historic problem facing messengers: *They're always in danger of being blamed for their messages.*

11

1960s HEROES AND VILLAINS:

" THE REAL ARRIVAL OF TELEVISION "

JOHN F. KENNEDY

Americans who lived through the 1960s have never forgotten where they were and what they were doing the day John F. Kennedy was shot. It was the first of four days in which the entire country shared in a tragedy that transformed a glamorous young president into a national hero.

"The assassination in Dallas," journalist and author Tom Wicker recalled thirty years later, "marked the real arrival of television, history's mightiest conveyor of images and moments. . . . [F]rom the moment the shots rang out in Dealey Plaza through the funeral services three days later, the networks stayed continuously on the air, steadily focused on the searing drama—bringing the nation together, as perhaps never before, in its time of shock and grief. Television, blazoning the events of the weekend on the memories of most Americans then living, became the national nervous system."

Television and John F. Kennedy had been closely linked ever since his victory in the first televised presidential debate. He was the first president to allow live

W*ashington Star* photo of Walter Cronkite interviewing President Kennedy for the first half-hour nightly network newscast aired on CBS, September 2, 1963. (Copyright © The *Washington Post.* Reprinted by permission of the D.C. Public Library)

TV coverage of his press conferences. When CBS and NBC began thirty-minute network newscasts, he was featured on the first nights. Kennedy and his wife, Jacqueline, were a made-for-television presidential couple—handsome, youthful, stylish. Kennedy's mastery of the medium made him the first television president.

Beginning on a sunny and cold January 20, 1961, Kennedy had established the tone of his administration with an inspiring inaugural address before a television audience of millions. At forty-three years of age, the youngest man elected president of the United States and the first Catholic, Kennedy stood without hat or overcoat, his breath frosted by the air. He cut a dashing figure as he summoned the nation to a New Frontier and announced to the world that "the torch has been passed to a new generation of Americans."

He issued a challenge that became an inspiration: "[A]sk not what your country can do for you—ask what you can do for your country."

Newsweek described inauguration day as "a spectacle made for television" and singled out "the most poignant" televised image of the day: "Mrs. Kennedy, a little pale, a little awed, but letting a proud Madonna-like smile caress her cheek as she watched her husband, the President, take his oath of office."

Harris Wofford, who worked closely with the Kennedys, recalled how the young president "rode the new wave of the electronic media. . . . With him and his family as the central political stars of the new medium, he completed the transition from the politics of radio to the politics of television."

The president captured the imagination of his fellow Americans. He fostered a spirit of hope, a sense of confidence, a determination to make the world a better place. He brought to Washington America's "best and brightest," as author David Halberstam described the people who served in Kennedy's administration.

Less than three years after the inauguration, on Friday afternoon, November 22, 1963, at 1:40 P.M. Eastern Standard Time, Walter Cronkite of CBS interrupted the TV soap opera *As the World Turns* to announce that the president had been shot in Dallas, Texas.

America stopped in its tracks. At times, nine out of ten Americans watched the ensuing four days of coverage, some for as many as eleven hours a day. The networks dropped all commercials for nonstop coverage: seventy-one hours and thirty-six minutes on NBC, sixty hours on ABC, fifty-five hours on CBS. The average home tuned in for 31.6 hours during the four days of grief.

TV interspersed live coverage of the aftermath with film of the assassination. Americans saw their president shot again and again and again. One stunning event followed another. Lee Harvey Oswald was captured as the man suspected of shooting Kennedy. The Dallas police held up a rifle for the TV cameras: "the murder weapon."

Five hours after the shooting, Air Force One landed in Washington, D.C., and the casket bearing the president descended by hydraulic lift. Jacqueline Kennedy followed the casket, her suit and stockings caked with blood. A somber Lyndon Johnson, newly sworn in as president, disembarked. "We have suffered a loss that cannot be weighed," he told the nation and promised: "I will do my best."

The following day, planeloads of world leaders, including twenty-three presidents and three reigning monarchs, began to arrive in Washington. Ninety-two nations sent delegations to pay their respects to America's fallen leader. On Sunday, Mrs. Kennedy and her children joined the procession to the Capitol, where the president's body would lie in state overnight.

Back in Dallas, NBC-TV cameras broadcast live as detectives escorted Oswald in handcuffs from the garage basement of the city jail on his way to the county jail. Suddenly, a heavy-set man in a gray fedora pushed his way into the picture. He was a Dallas nightclub owner named Jack Ruby. He fired a .38-caliber revolver point-blank at Oswald, mortally wounding him. The first murder ever televised live. Millions watched.

Shock was followed by grief when coverage switched back to Washington for the painful process of mourning the slain president. All night, NBC showed grieving men, women, and children filing by the coffin.

On Monday, nine out of ten TV homes tuned to what anchor David Brinkley called "our first genuinely national funeral, a death in our national family attended by every one of us." TV brought the funeral into the living rooms of all Americans. *Newsweek* called it a "shattering" experience.

Television had crossed a threshold. Viewing was no longer just escapism. It felt like a duty in times of national crisis. TV was the glue holding together a nation of indivisible viewers.

Television critic Marya Mannes described the experience as "total involvement": "I stayed before the set knowing—as millions knew—that I must give myself over entirely to an appalling tragedy, and that to evade it was a treason of the spirit."

Five years later, when assassins' bullets struck down the great civil rights leader Martin Luther King Jr. and another Kennedy, Americans again mourned via television. The numbing murders took place only two months apart—the first on April 4, 1968, on a Memphis, Tennessee, motel balcony, the second on June 5 in a Los Angeles hotel corridor.

On April 4, a sniper killed King with a single rifle shot fired from a rooming house across the street. The fatal shot set off what historian William Manchester described as "the worst outburst of arson, looting, and criminal activity in the nation's history." In 168 cities, 26,000 fires were set, 2,600 people arrested, 21,270 injured. In all, 55,000 troops were needed to restore order. It was a bloody period to the life of the 1964 recipient of the Nobel Peace Prize.

Local TV stations and the three networks broadcast full coverage of the repercussions. The seven-hour telecast of King's hero's funeral was beamed by satellite from his hometown of Atlanta, Georgia, to a worldwide audience.

Media historian Erik Barnouw described a TV audience of 120 million watching "spellbound as King's coffin, on a farm wagon drawn by two Georgia mules, moved toward the cemetery followed by crowds on foot—crowds estimated at two hundred thousand people."

An unprecedented day of national mourning was proclaimed, as CBS commentator Eric Sevareid reminded viewers: "It is doubtful if this nation has ever before gone into officially proclaimed mourning . . . over the death of a private citizen, and this man was the descendant of slaves."

America was still mourning Martin Luther King's loss, when on June 5, 1968, Robert F. Kennedy was also shot to death. A front-runner for the Democratic presidential nomination after President Johnson's withdrawal, he had just won the crucial California primary to select delegates for the Democratic National Convention. Americans found it hard to believe: another Kennedy assassinated.

Within minutes of the shooting, TV showed the pandemonium at the scene. Kennedy and five others lay on the floor, bleeding from the eight shots fired by a Jordanian immigrant, Sirhan Bishara Sirhan. A bullet had entered Kennedy's brain, mortally wounding him. The others were wounded slightly.

"Once more," media historian Barnouw wrote, "hundreds of millions of television viewers witnessed a ritual beyond belief." St. Patrick's Cathedral in New York City overflowed with everyday people who revered Kennedy and came to pay final respects. The powerful and the famous were present at a funeral service in which the surviving Kennedy brother, Edward, delivered the eulogy in a trembling voice.

The body was taken to Pennsylvania Station to travel by train to Washington, D.C., so Robert could be buried near his brother John. The crowds along the train route were so dense that the three-hour trip took eight hours.

Historian John Morton Blum summarized the double loss suffered by the United States in 1968 and shared via television: "In April, King; in June, Kennedy—the two most understanding, the two most magnetic, the two most needed Americans were gone."

Millions of TV viewers became mourners. They

went to the funeral, an experience magnified and made more dramatic by TV close-ups and solemn commentary by trusted news anchors. Americans were not mourning leaders somewhere in the distance on a platform. They were mourning murdered husbands and fathers and seeing the tears of their wives and children.

The TV experience turned political assassinations into personal losses as immediate as a death in the family.

12

1960s EYE-OPENERS:

" ONE GIANT LEAP FOR MANKIND "

THE *APOLLO 11* MOONSHOT

"It's just a little jump," astronaut Neil A. Armstrong said as he stood on the last rung of a nine-rung ladder 238,000 miles from planet Earth.

Back on Earth, hundreds of millions were watching on live television, probably as many as a billion people. In the United States, 94 percent of all TV homes were tuned in. In Washington, President Richard M. Nixon was glued to a portable TV in his office. In Rome, Pope Paul VI followed the event hour by hour. In Las Vegas, casino operators set up color TVs in the gambling rooms and asked gamblers to "refrain from their pursuit of jackpots" during the telecast.

In the New York studio of CBS-TV, famed news anchor Walter Cronkite said in his running commentary: "So there's a foot on the moon, stepping down on the moon. If he's testing that first step, he must be stepping down on the moon at this point."

At 10:56 P.M. Eastern Daylight Time on July 20, 1969, Armstrong's left foot made the first human foot–

Astronaut Edwin E. "Buzz" Aldrin Jr. and the *Apollo 11* lunar module, *Eagle*, photographed by Neil A. Armstrong on the moon, July 20, 1969. (Courtesy of NASA)

print on the moon. He jumped into history with the words, "That's one small step for a man, one giant leap for mankind."

Just before stepping down from the ladder, Armstrong pulled a cord to open the lens of a black-and-white TV camera. In 1.3 seconds, the time it took for light to travel from the moon to the Earth, the TV signal traveled to a receiving station in Parkes, Australia, and was relayed around the world.

Armstrong's "small step" climaxed a project born 2,978 days earlier when President John F. Kennedy told Congress on May 25, 1961: "I believe that this nation should commit itself to achieving the goal, before this decade is out, of landing a man on the moon and returning him safely to earth." With these words, the United States launched a space race. The object was to reach the moon before its cold war rival, the Soviet Union. Kennedy staked national prestige on a moon landing.

TV provided a stage for showing the world what American ingenuity and initiative could do. The moon project provided TV with a history-making story that was filled with drama, suspense, and fantastic, eye-opening images.

The National Aeronautics and Space Administration (NASA) spent $5 billion a year for eight years and reached the goal with less than six months left in the decade. This monumental effort was compared to building the pyramids of Egypt. Hundreds of thousands of people worked on the project, millions of hours of engineering time were logged. At the peak of the space race, 20,000 industrial and university contractors employed 420,000 people on NASA's behalf.

Before attempting the *Apollo 11* moon mission, NASA had to develop space vehicles and train people to pilot them. From 1961 to 1963, Project Mercury tested space pilots, dubbed astronauts, in solo flights orbiting the earth for up to thirty-four hours. In 1965 and 1966, the Gemini program of ten flights sent two astronauts into orbit for as long as two weeks. Gemini also perfected techniques for two vehicles to rendezvous and dock and for astronauts to "walk" in space.

At the beginning of the Apollo flights, the moon program was almost stopped short by a disaster. In January 1967, a fire in the *Apollo 1* capsule during a flight simulation killed the three-man crew. Then in March, a Soviet capsule, *Soyuz 1,* crashed on reentry, killing a veteran cosmonaut. These were jarring reminders of the dangers of space travel.

Apollo missions didn't get off the ground until twenty-one months later. When the first Apollo flight orbited the earth 163 times, television viewers shared the astronauts' view of Earth from orbit. *Apollo 8,* the first spacecraft to go into orbit around the moon, sent back the first TV broadcast from lunar orbit and transmitted spectacular views of the moon on Christmas Eve 1968. Mission by mission, each Apollo prepared the way for the moon landing by testing technology, routes—and astronauts. Finally, everything was ready.

At 9:32 A.M. on Wednesday, July 16, 1969, a thirty-six-story-high Saturn 5 rocket was fired at Cape Kennedy's launch complex 39A. It sent into space the *Apollo 11* command vessel, *Columbia,* and the lunar module, *Eagle.* Aboard were the crew's civilian commander, Neil A. Armstrong, and two Air Force officers, Colonel Edwin E. "Buzz" Aldrin Jr. and Lieutenant

Colonel Michael Collins.

On Friday afternoon in space, Armstrong and Aldrin crept through a tunnel connecting *Columbia* and the *Eagle*.

On Sunday, Armstrong and Aldrin separated the *Eagle* and headed for their landing site on the moon's Sea of Tranquility. At 4:17 P.M. Eastern Daylight Time, Armstrong announced, "The *Eagle* has landed."

Cronkite in New York was at a loss for words. He exclaimed, "Oh, boy!"

Next came the historic footstep and Armstrong's description of the moon's surface—"fine and powdery. . . . I only go in a fraction of an inch, maybe an eighth of an inch, but I can see the footprints of my boots and the treads in the fine, sandy particles."

Nineteen minutes later, Aldrin joined Armstrong, and they set up a TV camera so viewers on planet Earth could see them bound around the moon collecting rock samples. They planted a three-by-five-foot nylon U.S. flag stiffened at the top by an aluminum rod so it would seem on television to blow in a breeze, though the lunar surface is windless. The world watched Aldrin salute the flag.

President Nixon talked directly to the astronauts by radio-telephone. On television, he appeared on one-half of a split screen, the astronauts on the other. He couldn't resist the comment that "this certainly has to be the most historic phone call ever made."

In a proclamation, Nixon noted that exploration was no longer "a lonely enterprise," as in the past. Now the astronauts' achievement could be shared: "Television brings the moment of discovery into our homes and makes us all participants."

After following *Apollo 11* at every stage, television had gone all-out on the day of the moon landing. CBS and NBC canceled their regular programs for thirty-one hours starting at 11 A.M. Sunday, ABC for thirty hours beginning at noon.

"To fill the hours, the networks pulled out all the stops and scheduled an impressive array of names," *Time* magazine reported. The array ranged from scientists to science-fiction writers and from actors and poets reading on screen to entertainers talking about the moon and romance. For the occasion, ABC commissioned the famed musician Duke Ellington to write and perform a special composition, "Moon Maiden."

While some scientists questioned the need to send a man rather than a machine to the moon, no one could argue with the manned mission's tremendous psychological, emotional, and political impact, or with television's dominant role in intensifying the public's interest in the race to the moon.

The televised *Apollo 11* moon trip filled Americans with pride at home and built U.S. prestige abroad. Media historian Barnouw pointed out that "the television spectacular was an epoch-making success. . . . A key element was the American willingness to allow live coverage of what might turn into disaster. For hundreds of millions of people throughout the world, watching via satellites, the unspoken possibility of disaster must have been ever present. Against the background of this peril, the calm assurance had an epic quality. To such men, could anything be impossible?"

When *Columbia* splashed down safely on Thursday, July 24, in the Pacific Ocean, whistles blew, church bells rang, and motorists honked their horns loud and

clear all over the United States and in cities around the world.

At the end of America's turbulent 1960s, there was poetic justice in making "one giant leap for mankind." It reminded Americans that they had the resources and know-how to meet great challenges. It was a reassuring and welcome relief for television viewers to share a moment of triumph after a decade of adversity.

HOME sweet home

PART 3 THE 1970s

13

THE 1970s:

" THE AMERICAN GAZE TURNED INWARD "

At first, the 1970s felt like the 1960s. Many Americans, protesting and rebelling, were still out to transform the world and their country.

Then the mood changed.

Americans switched focus—from helping the world to helping themselves, from doing good to making good. Rather than trying to improve society, they tried to improve themselves. And they worked hard at it.

In an "epitaph" for the decade, *Time* magazine stated: "Mostly the air in the '70s was thick with a sense of aftermath, of public passions spent and consciences bewildered. The American gaze turned inward."

As early as 1971, ex-Beatle John Lennon began singing "The Dream Is Over" and telling his fans that he had stopped believing in President Kennedy and the other heroes of the 1960s. Instead he sang: "I just believe in me."

Americans tried to pick up their spirits by wearing happy faces—yellow buttons that displayed two black dots for eyes and a black half circle to represent a smile. Twenty million buttons were sold in 1971.

It was a forced smile. Inflation was making it harder to pay the bills as prices went up and salaries didn't. In 1973, Americans even had to wait in long lines to buy gas for their cars because of an Arab oil embargo.

Detroit, car manufacturing capital of the world, was going downhill; Americans were buying Japanese cars. In the 1950s and 1960s, "Made in Japan" meant a product was cheap and second-rate; now it meant better than American-made.

In 1973, the United States had its first trade deficit in eighty-five years, and for the first time since their inception, national polls found that half of all Americans expected life to get worse. By 1975 the number of unemployed American workers reached almost 8 million, and the unemployment rate rose to the highest it had been since 1940, the last year of the Great Depression.

It was also a decade of violence and of victims. Violent crimes increased by 60 percent between 1971 and 1980. After a wave of plane hijackings, all 531 U.S. airports began screening passengers with metal detectors.

It was almost as if you couldn't tell who was a hero and who was a villain anymore. The nation was shocked by the illegal acts of both the vice president and the president. Vice President Spiro T. Agnew resigned on October 10, 1973, after making a deal with the U.S. Justice Department on charges that he had taken bribes while governor of Maryland. He pleaded "no contest" to a lesser charge of tax evasion. To replace him, Nixon nominated and the Senate approved Gerald R. Ford, the first vice president ever to be appointed, not elected.

The distinguished Yale University historian John Morton Blum has rendered a harsh verdict on Agnew:

"He had admitted his guilt and copped a plea, just like the cheap crook he was."

Months later, faced with the Watergate scandal over illegal wiretapping, a break-in, and cover-up, President Richard M. Nixon went on television from Disney World to plead his case with the American people. "I'm not a crook," he told them. This time, he didn't win over the public as he had in his 1952 Checkers speech.

By the time Nixon resigned on August 9, 1974, rather than face impeachment, only 14 percent of Americans expressed confidence in him. His successor, President Gerald Ford, saved him from criminal prosecution by pardoning him. The *New York Times* called it "an unconscionable act."

Then things got worse for the United States. It lost a war for the first time in its history. Play by play, viewers watched the humbling of America in Vietnam. Network coverage was unstinting. The three networks each had a staff of about thirty in Vietnam, including five to six reporter-camera teams. Their coverage saturated the country.

By 1974, the network evening news was carried by 191 affiliated ABC stations, 194 CBS stations, and 210 NBC stations. TV was in 97 percent of U.S. households in 1975, 98 percent at the end of the decade.

Behind the scenes, technology improved television coverage. In the mid-1970s, video cameras replaced film cameras to usher in electronic news gathering (ENG). These small, relatively light cameras captured both pictures and sound on videotape. Editing could be done electronically and immediately. By comparison, film required a separate machine for sound recording and then had to be developed for an hour or more before editing. ENG expanded coverage and put stories on the air faster than ever.

Meanwhile, TV had a story to tell that didn't have the drama of Vietnam and Watergate. It was the story of how Americans felt about themselves and how they were turning their "gaze inward." They were feeling disillusioned.

It happened gradually. No single event heralded the demise of youthful dreams, of optimism about transforming the world, of faith in national leaders. Television told that story with individual reports on the evening news.

On college campuses, career planning began to replace activism. It became important to "dress for success." Twice as many law and business degrees were earned in 1973 as five years earlier. At the tenth reunion booklet of Harvard College's class of '63, dozens of one-time radicals described what they were doing in the 1970s: taking care of themselves and getting ahead.

Americans made a best-seller of a book that said it all in the title, *Looking Out for No. 1*. A best-seller on finding happiness announced *I'm O.K.—You're O.K.* and guided readers into self-acceptance.

Hit songs expressed the country's mood: "Bridge Over Troubled Waters," "Feelings," "You're So Vain," "All by Myself."

Americans gulped down bottled water imported from France, and 20 million of them took up jogging for their health. (In 1970, 127 runners signed up for the New York City Marathon; in 1979, 11,533.) A "human potential movement" spread from coast to coast and involved all kinds of quick-fix programs for people to "find" themselves.

In the 1970s, life in America became a private enterprise. Disillusioned, backing away from great causes, mistrusting their leaders, Americans seemed to focus most on taking care of number one.

Many Americans who experienced those years agreed with the label coined for the 1970s by social critic Tom Wolfe: the *Me Decade*.

14

1970s CONFRONTATION:

" MY GOD! MY GOD! THEY'RE KILLING US! "

THE KENT STATE KILLINGS

On May 4, 1970, a noisy crowd of student antiwar protesters confronted a line of jittery National Guardsmen wearing gas masks and holding M-1 rifles loaded with live ammunition.

The National Guardsmen had been sent to the Kent State campus in Ohio to restore peace during a weekend of stormy protests that included the burning of the Reserve Officers' Training Corps (ROTC) building.

Suddenly, at 12:24 P.M., without warning, the guardsmen fired a salvo of sixty-one bullets in thirteen bloody seconds.

In the awesome silence that followed, Ron Steele, a freshman, screamed, "My God! My God! They're killing us!"

In the Old Testament, young David killed Goliath the giant with five smooth stones and a sling. But in Ohio, when students threw rocks against National Guardsmen pointing semiautomatic rifles, the giant won.

Eleven students were wounded, four killed. William Schroeder Jr., nineteen, had stopped to watch

John Filo's Pulitzer Prize-winning photograph of a young woman grieving over the body of student protester Jeffery Miller, killed by National Guardsmen during an antiwar demonstration on the Kent State University campus, May 4, 1970. (Courtesy of John Paul Filo)

the protesters. Sandra Scheuer, twenty, was walking to class. On the previous day, Allison Krause, nineteen, had placed a flower in the barrel of a guardsman's rifle, saying, "Flowers are better than bullets." The fourth victim, Jeffrey Miller, had been among the protesters. As he lay facedown, lifeless, a young woman rushed forward and knelt beside his body. She uttered what student photographer John Filo described as "a God-awful scream."

Filo captured the scene in a wrenching photograph that was seen around the world on the front pages of newspapers and news magazines and on television screens. The media seized upon this single image to depict what had happened at Kent State.

The killings stunned viewers and fanned the flames of protest. "Antiwar fever, which President Richard Nixon had skillfully reduced to a tolerable level last fall, surged upward again to a point unequaled since Lyndon Johnson was driven from the White House," *Time* magazine reported.

Of all the extensive media coverage, the May 5 NBC evening newscast was the most dramatic. First, the Filo photograph filled the screen accompanied by seven seconds of narration. Then for an additional twelve seconds the photograph remained on the screen, a frozen image. There was no sound, no motion, only the photograph "screaming" before millions of viewers.

The Kent State confrontation had been one of the nationwide campus protests against President Nixon's decision to demonstrate that the United States was not "a pitiful, helpless giant," as he put it. In a televised address on April 30, 1970, Nixon announced that he had sent U.S. forces into Vietnam's neighbor, Cambodia, to expel North Vietnamese troops and to protect Cambodia's pro-Western government against a Communist takeover.

It was the last thing Americans wanted: U.S. military involvement in another Southeast Asian country. The invasion contradicted Nixon's previous claims that the Vietnam War was winding down. Moreover, Nixon went beyond his constitutional powers as president by invading a country without the approval of the U.S. Congress.

Nixon's speech, followed by the Kent State killings, triggered unprecedented campus unrest, nationwide. Two-thirds of the colleges in New England closed. California closed all 121 branches of its state college system. By the end of May, 415 colleges and universities had been disrupted. Historian William Manchester called it "the first general student strike in the country's history, and it was entirely spontaneous."

Kent State created a ripple effect. Network and local coverage of demonstrations, student strikes, and takeovers and burnings of buildings made more and more Americans ask: Was Vietnam worth these young lives at home as well as on the battlefield? The controversy tore the country apart.

Nixon had miscalculated. The Cambodian invasion was a failure both in Southeast Asia and in the United States. It did not clear the Communists out of Cambodia. Worse still, as *Time* magazine pointed out, even if it had succeeded, the invasion could never make up for the damage to American morale and solidarity.

The Senate reacted to the president's acting without their consent by passing a resolution demanding that U.S. troops leave Cambodia immediately. The president, under pressure, promised that the troops would leave within three to seven weeks. Five months later, a special presidential commission warned of student violence if the United States didn't end the war in Vietnam. Tom Wicker, who as a *New York Times* columnist was a firsthand observer, has recalled the impact of media coverage: "To many Americans, the day of revolution may have seemed at hand, not least because the attention of newspapers and television naturally was on the exploding campuses, not on the rest of the nation going routinely about its business."

Television broadcast the antiwar message loudly and clearly. It gave students worldwide visibility, and the attention made their protests important and powerful. The country began to wonder if they might be right.

The government was forced to pay attention to the message blaring from televisions across the country: ONE, TWO, THREE, FOUR, WE DON'T WANT YOUR ——ING WAR!

15

1970s POLITICS:

" MAKING THE ABSTRACT...SHOCKINGLY REAL "

THE WATERGATE INVESTIGATION

On the evening of August 8, 1974, an estimated 110 million Americans watched as TV cameras in the Oval Office of the White House zeroed in on their president's face. Only the first moon landing had attracted more U.S. viewers (125 million).

They were witnessing a historic act. Richard Milhous Nixon, looking tense and defeated, announced his resignation and ended his twenty-eight-year political career as the first president of the United States ever driven from office.

In a sixteen-minute speech, Nixon acknowledged that he had lost the support of the country. He told his TV audience that he was serving "the interests of America" by resigning as president. After months of controversy, exposure, and revelations about his misuse and abuse of the office of president, he was leaving in disgrace to avoid impeachment.

Television was there as it had been throughout

Closeup taken from a TV screen of President Nixon announcing the release of
transcripts of conversations tape-recorded in his office to the Senate committee
investigating the Watergate cover-up, April 29, 1974. (Library of Congress)

Nixon's political career. It had saved him in his famous Checkers speech and worked against him in the presidential debate with Kennedy. Television had helped build his popularity as a get-tough opponent of communism, particularly in network coverage of the 1959 "kitchen debate" with Russian leader Nikita Khrushchev. Nixon had stood up to tough-talking Khrushchev in an argument over free enterprise in a model kitchen at a U.S. exhibition in Moscow.

When Nixon went to Communist China in 1972 to establish relations in his great foreign-policy achievement, TV had dramatized the event by showing the leaders of the two countries toasting each other. *Newsweek* had called coverage of Nixon's arrival in China "the season's best network TV show." When Nixon signed a nuclear arms treaty with the Soviet Union in 1972, he had once again received full network attention.

While Nixon was always ready to use the media in any way he could, he mistrusted journalists. He even had an "enemies" list of the ones he mistrusted most. It seemed appropriate, almost inevitable, that the media played a major role in his downfall.

It all started with the arrest on June 17, 1972, of five burglars at the Democratic National Committee headquarters in Washington's luxurious Watergate apartment complex. Hence the label: the Watergate scandal.

The "burglars" were hired by Nixon's 1972 reelection committee to install wiretaps on the Democrats' telephones. They were part of an underhanded operation that included spying, "dirty tricks," wiretapping, and intimidation.

Two newspaper reporters, Bob Woodward and Carl Bernstein of the *Washington Post*, led the way in bringing the scandal to light. They uncovered an all-out effort by members of Nixon's staff to cover up the burglary. They even had evidence that implicated the president himself.

The president became personally involved six days after the burglary by participating in the cover-up of the connection between the burglary and his reelection committee. He didn't want the truth to come out and thereby hurt his 1972 reelection campaign.

The heart of the Watergate scandal wasn't the burglary. It was the cover-up, which resulted in a web of illegal acts that ranged far and wide through the federal government. By the time of Nixon's resignation, as *Newsweek* magazine reported, the "scandals" of Watergate had "dishonored the Vice Presidency, the Cabinet, the White House staff, the FBI, the CIA, the Department of Justice, the courts and finally the Presidency itself."

The subsequent investigation not only proved the cover-up but found that Nixon and his staff had been involved in espionage, sabotage, and their own private police operation. The president of the United States and his closest associates were caught breaking the law.

Time magazine called Watergate the "nation's greatest scandal and journalism's longest-running political story." But it was network TV that expanded the shocked audience from Washington, D.C., to the entire nation. In his memoirs, Nixon later couldn't resist charging that it had been a "media assault."

Not surprisingly, as media historian Edward Bliss Jr. notes, the investigative reporting of Woodward and

Bernstein put the *Washington Post* "first on Nixon's hate list," with CBS second. CBS earned its place on the list during the 1972 campaign.

On October 27, two weeks before election day, Walter Cronkite devoted fourteen minutes of his twenty-two-minute newscast to an analysis of how the president's men were involved in Watergate. A second Cronkite report followed four days later. It was shortened to eight minutes after a close Nixon associate phoned CBS to denounce the first report as unfair.

Nixon never hid his mistrust of the press, nor did he hesitate to put pressure on it. In fact, at the beginning of the 1972 campaign Nixon told one of his speech writers that it was "very important" that the media "be effectively discredited."

As it turned out, the Watergate scandal had almost no effect on Nixon's reelection campaign. On election day, Nixon overwhelmed his Democratic opponent, George McGovern. Six out of ten voters cast their ballots for Nixon, who won everywhere except in Massachusetts and the District of Columbia.

It wasn't until after Nixon began his second term as president that front-page stories and network news coverage of Watergate set the stage for what has become American politics' ultimate arena of public exposure: televised congressional hearings. In this instance, a select committee of the Senate was set up to investigate Watergate under the chairmanship of Senator Sam J. Ervin Jr. of North Carolina.

On May 17, 1973, the Senate's Select Committee on Presidential Campaign Activities, known popularly as the Watergate Committee, began nationally televised hearings that lasted thirty-seven days and filled 319 hours of daytime viewing. Fans of soap operas and game shows deserted their favorite programs to watch what *Newsweek* called "pure theater . . . an unqualified smash."

Time magazine pinpointed the role of TV in the hearings: "As cameras whir in the ornate, chandelier-strung Caucus Room, television, while still a spectator, at last is doing what it does best: making what seems abstract or exaggerated or just plain irrelevant on paper appear shockingly real."

Viewers were fascinated. They watched witnesses link the president to the cover-up and were stunned to learn that Nixon secretly taped private discussions held in his office. Nixon then roused suspicions of his own guilt by withholding the tapes. Nixon's troubles continued to mount. A special Watergate prosecutor, Archibald Cox, was appointed by the attorney general at the insistence of the Senate Judiciary Committee. When Cox demanded the tapes, Nixon had him fired, creating another media firestorm.

Cox's successor, Leon Jaworski, also demanded the tapes and brought criminal charges against Nixon's closest associates. Eventually, nineteen Nixon aides and associates, including two cabinet members, went to prison for their part in Watergate.

In February 1974, the House of Representatives authorized its Judiciary Committee to discuss impeachment. If approved by the committee, articles of impeachment would be the first step toward removing Nixon from office.

Next, the House of Representatives would vote on articles of impeachment. Once impeached by the House, the president would be tried by the Senate. A two-thirds vote on the charges would be required for the Senate to convict and remove the president from office.

During March and April of 1974, while the Senate committee's staff accumulated forty volumes of material, Nixon still resisted demands to turn over more tapes of conversations in his office. Instead, he released written transcripts, claiming in a nationally televised speech that they contained everything "relevant . . . the rough as well as the smooth. . . . The President has nothing to hide."

Historian John Morton Blum has bluntly described the claim as "a bald lie."

On July 24, 1974, Nixon lost his last major Watergate battle when the Supreme Court ordered him to surrender the tapes to Special Prosecutor Jaworski. Nixon's own words convicted him. Even diehard supporters deserted him when they learned what was on the tapes: Nixon joining, guiding, participating in the illegal cover-up.

One particularly damning conversation took place between Nixon and presidential counsel John Dean on March 21, 1973. The media had a field day with it. It was about paying off the Watergate burglars to keep quiet and not implicate the White House. Dean told the president that it would cost a million dollars.

The president answered: "We could get that. On the money, if you need the money we can get that. You could get a million dollars. You could get it in cash. I know where it could be gotten. It is not easy, but it could be done."

The next television drama centered on the Judiciary Committee of the House of Representatives. For the first

122

time, the House authorized broadcast of a committee meeting. Previously, only congressional hearings had been broadcast. The authorization took television another step forward in bringing the political process into the living room. It was going to show a congressional committee at work, debating, discussing, deciding.

There was more dignity than drama in the televised result. This was appropriate in view of the historic action. Thirty-eight committee members went before the cameras to explain how they stood on Watergate. Each had a turn in the spotlight for fifteen minutes. The close-ups said more than the words: This was a serious, solemn occasion; this was a painful and agonizing decision.

On July 27, the cameras recorded the resounding House committee vote in favor of impeachment. Nixon was accused of obstructing justice, abusing power, and defying congressional subpoenas. An ordinary citizen convicted of such crimes could face up to thirty years in jail. The next step would be for the committee to turn over the approved articles to the full House of Representatives for a vote.

Finally, Nixon faced the fact that he was all through. The evidence was against him. The House of Representatives would surely approve the articles of impeachment, and the Senate would probably then convict him.

Nixon avoided the humiliation and disgrace of impeachment by resigning. His last official act was a one-sentence letter dated August 9, 1974: "I hereby resign the Office of President of the United States."

Nearly fifteen years later, Nixon added a postscript to Watergate and a testimonial to the power of television in American politics and government. This came in

published advice to another Republican president, George Bush, just before his inauguration in 1989: "Of all the institutions arrayed with and against a president, none controls his fate more than television."

16

1970s WAR:

" A HOLE IN THE NATIONAL PSYCHE "

THE VIETNAM WAR: WITHDRAWAL

The United States, the Free World's superpower, sent more than three million men and women into the Vietnam War; 57,690 were killed and more than 300,000 wounded fighting to save South Vietnam from a Communist takeover.

But after fourteen years, after billions of dollars spent, and after all the bloodshed, the United States gave up the fight. At the last minute, the Americans remaining in Vietnam had to run for their lives as the Communist forces of North Vietnam closed in on Saigon, the capital of South Vietnam.

The final collapse was "captured in astounding television pictures," veteran journalists Robert J. Donovan and Ray Scherer noted in their study of TV news.

At the end, U.S. officials and their South Vietnamese staffers climbed to the embassy roof in Saigon to escape. Marine helicopters picked them up and flew them to ships of the U.S. Seventh Fleet waiting offshore.

An Air America helicopter conducts a last-minute evacuation from the roof of the U.S. embassy in Saigon, April 29, 1975. (UPI/Bettmann)

It was a frantic scene. Men and women scrambled up a narrow stairway to the cramped landing pad where the helicopter waited, its propellers whirring. A solitary figure at the top of the ladder strained to help the evacuees into the chopper. Down below, men and women crowded around the ladder struggling to be next.

"Finally," as described by Donovan and Scherer, "the last of the helicopters pulled away from a sea of upraised arms of South Vietnamese trying to catch hold. On television screens in America the pictures caused a humiliation that was not to be assuaged until Iraq's surrender in the Persian Gulf War sixteen years later."

The image of the last CH-46 helicopter lifting off the embassy roof "burned a hole in the national psyche" according to *New York Times* political commentator R. W. Apple Jr.

The last-minute evacuation was the painful climax of prolonged U.S. efforts to get free of the Vietnam quagmire, beginning with peace talks in May 1968. After Nixon became president in 1969, he undertook a policy of increased bombing in Vietnam while facing escalating antiwar feelings at home. On November 15, 1969, antiwar sentiment peaked when 250,000 people marched on Washington in opposition to the war.

Public support for Nixon's handling of the war drained away. By April 1971, support sank to 34 percent, down from 65 percent only fifteen months earlier. More than half of all Americans polled felt that the Vietnam War had been a mistake in the first place.

In May 1971, the United States proposed a cease-fire and a deadline for its withdrawal from Vietnam in exchange for the return of American prisoners of war. After months of frustrating negotiations, a peace agreement, signed on January 27, 1973, ended the longest war in U.S. history. The last U.S. combat soldier left Vietnam in March 1973.

But the fighting didn't stop. The South Vietnamese tried to battle on, relying on continued U.S. military aid and nine thousand American advisers. But the struggle was doomed. Their forces lacked the leadership and the determination to withstand the North Vietnamese.

In January 1975 North Vietnamese leaders mounted the war's final offensive, expecting victory to take two years. To their surprise, it took only a few months. The South Vietnamese Army just seemed to fall apart.

Saigon was on the verge of collapse in late April, forcing the United States to begin Operation Frequent Wind, an aerial evacuation of American advisers and South Vietnamese officials. It began at Saigon's airport, where thousands were flown out of South Vietnam, and ended on the U.S. embassy roof with the last helicopter lifting off at 5 A.M. on April 30, 1975.

The final message to Washington from the embassy said: "It's been a long and hard fight and we have lost. . . . Saigon signing off."

By the time official word of Saigon's unconditional surrender reached New York at 10:30 in the evening, CBS and NBC were already on the air with special programs about the end of the Vietnam War. ABC broadcast a special ninety-minute program one hour later.

"There's no way," said Walter Cronkite, concluding the CBS TV special, "to capture the suffering and the grief of our own nation from the most divisive conflict since our own Civil War."

Looking back, television played a major role in tearing America apart over the Vietnam War. It fueled the controversy for Americans on both sides, those who supported the war and those who opposed it. Robert J. Donovan and Ray Scherer concluded, "The more that was pictured on television, the more the opinions of both sides hardened. Year after year television showed scenes of the war to the American people and kept the argument going."

Without television, the war would have remained remote, something to read about and push into the background. With television, millions of viewers saw the price of war in the deaths of young Americans and in the pain and suffering of the Vietnamese. Every Thursday evening they watched the casualty count on all three TV networks. In stark numbers, they saw the tally of Americans killed and wounded in Vietnam grow week after week. They also witnessed more and more demonstrations against the war by students and members of the clergy and even returning veterans.

On April 18, 1971, the Vietnam Veterans Against the War demonstrated in Washington. Veterans in wheelchairs denounced the war and announced that they were returning their medals for heroism. They told the national TV audience that they were ashamed of having fought in Vietnam.

With its coverage of the Vietnam War, television demonstrated both its ability to inform Americans about a story and its ability to make the audience feel what was happening. On television, the news was vivid, immediate, and emotionally powerful, all the more so since the Vietnam War coincided with the introduction in 1965 of color to network news.

Color heightened the effect of war coverage. As media historian Barnouw pointed out, "Mud and blood were indistinguishable in black and white; in color, blood was blood. In color, misty Vietnamese landscapes hung with indescribable beauty behind gory actions."

In a discussion of television's role, General William Westmoreland, who commanded U.S. forces in Vietnam, complained that no one would have known about the war had it not been for television.

Robert Northshield of CBS, who was listening, had an immediate reply. He shouted: "Then thank God for television!" He was speaking for journalists' determination to report the story whether the audience wanted to see it or not. He was upholding the argument that democracy is in danger when government operates in secret and its actions, including blunders, are hidden from view.

On the question of reliability in covering Vietnam, historian William Hammond made a significant point when he compared journalists with the government as sources of information. He pointed out that the reports on television and in the press "were still often more accurate than the public statements of the administration in portraying the situation in Vietnam."

Speaking for all journalists, the respected *New York Times* columnist James Reston characterized reporters as "more honest with the American people than the officials."

Even when critics singled out TV news as too brief, superficial, and obsessed with what is visual and dramatic at the expense of in-depth reporting, they never denied the impact of TV. If TV had made little difference, then people in power would not have bothered to criticize and complain.

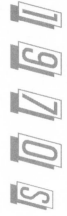

In Vietnam, the U.S. government and the military were frustrated because they could not control reporters as they would have if Congress had declared war. Technically speaking, U.S. forces were in Vietnam as "guests" to help the South Vietnamese government. Officially, it was never America's war, so there was no military censorship. Reporters could pursue their stories and send them back to the United States without submitting them for government approval.

Therefore, Vietnam, the first televised war, was also the first uncensored war. Television had free reign to show that war was hell. The effect of watching the war on television could even have greater impact than being there. This happened to a member of the Vietnamese National Assembly, Tran Ngoc Chau, while he was visiting Washington, D.C.

As a former province chief, he had been in the middle of the Vietnam War. Yet he found the images that he saw on the TV screen "horrifying, cruel and tragic" beyond what he had experienced firsthand. Stunned, he wrote in his diary:

"Over more than 20 years, I had seen many bodies with fresh blood of Asians, whites, blacks, by the dozens, the hundreds. Sometimes I hated it, sometimes I was moved, but never before was I so moved, did I hate it so much, was I so fed up as at this time, even though the scene was only brought by television."

17

1970s EYE-OPENERS:

" AN ASSAULT ON PRESS FREEDOM HAD BEEN REPELLED "

"THE SELLING OF THE PENTAGON"

A rocket fired by a jet plane streaks across the sky. . . . There is a series of shattering explosions. . . . Suddenly, soldiers in combat gear are running and firing their rifles. . . .

CBS correspondent Roger Mudd informed TV viewers that this was not a report from South Vietnam, but from North Carolina, where the U.S. military was putting on a show for civilians sitting in the stands. Then the scene cut to members of the U.S. Army special fighting unit, the Green Berets, demonstrating hand-to-hand combat in New Jersey for a thousand schoolchildren. The camera focused on the boys jumping on each other and trying out the kicks and karate chops used by the Green Berets. At another demonstration, business executives

Representative Harley O. Staggers, Chairman of the House Commerce Committee, faces TV cameras after Congress refused to cite CBS President Frank Stanton and his network for contempt of Congress for refusing to reveal sources of material used in the "Selling of the Pentagon" documentary, July 13, 1971. (UPI/Bettman)

described on camera the thrill of firing machine guns and tank cannons, courtesy of the army.

From the start, Mudd made clear what the report was about: how the U.S. military used taxpayers' money to sell itself to the American public. Hence the title of the controversial documentary, "The Selling of the Pentagon," seen Tuesday evening, February 23, 1971, in two hundred U.S. cities. Eleven months in the making, the sixty-minute program accused the military of carrying on a nationwide campaign to brainwash the public with pro-military messages.

The broadcast created a firestorm.

Before it was over, more than five hundred viewers had phoned, half of them outraged by what they saw. The first denunciation came after only fourteen minutes, when a caller accused narrator Mudd of being "an agent of a foreign power." After the halfway point, a U.S. Air Force colonel called to say, "The next time I see Mudd I'm going to take the nose off his face."

By criticizing the U.S. military, the documentary outraged supporters of the Vietnam War. By spotlighting the propaganda efforts of the military, the documentary outraged the opponents of the war. There was plenty of outrage to go around.

The material in the documentary already had been debated in Congress and revealed in books without winning much public attention—until TV broadcast its eye-opening documentary. *Time* magazine joined TV reviewers in praising the program and CBS's courage. It called the documentary "a landmark of sorts . . . a convincing demonstration that when it comes to stage-managing the news, no one tries harder or succeeds better than the government itself."

In the CBS documentary, the Pentagon admitted spending $30 million a year on public relations. Then correspondent Mudd cited a report by an independent foundation, the Twentieth Century Fund, that the real amount was closer to $190 million. That was $40 million more than all three networks together spent in an entire year to cover the news.

The cameras filmed a "mad minute" when multiple weapons were fired simultaneously during a public demonstration. A weapons officer priced the single display at $2 million.

The U.S. military was joined in its condemnation of CBS by supporters in the U.S. Congress, especially the chairman of the House Armed Services Committee, Representative F. Edward Hebert of Louisiana. Hebert had previously called network television "the most vicious instrument in America today." He said "The Selling of the Pentagon" was "one of the most un-American things I've ever seen . . . on the tube, the greatest disservice to the military I've ever seen on television, and I've seen some pretty bad stuff."

Congressional committees set out to investigate the fairness and accuracy of the program. Subpoenas were issued for unused film and records connected with the program. When CBS refused to turn them over, the issue of freedom of the press for television took over the spotlight.

In the end, CBS prevailed. It did not give in to congressional demands. "An assault on press freedom had been repelled," media historian Edward Bliss Jr. noted.

The documentary raised such a furor that it was rebroadcast a month later with a twenty-minute postscript that included the views of Vice President Spiro

Agnew and CBS News President Richard Salant. The second time around the program drew 14 million viewers, half as many as the first time.

"The Selling of the Pentagon" was *proactive* television. Rather than limit itself to reporting events as they happen, CBS took the initiative in exploring the issue of Pentagon propaganda. Such documentaries represent the power and glory of TV journalism: the power to influence public opinion and affect government action, and the glory of captivating audiences.

As Martin Mayer noted in his thought-provoking book *About Television*, "The documentaries are what television *does*—everything else is more or less forced upon the medium by events or availabilities."

"The Selling of the Pentagon" was only one among many powerful TV documentaries in the 1970s, including "Pensions: The Broken Promise" broadcast on NBC, September 12, 1972. The program warned that many private pension plans could run out of money. Fred W. Friendly, one of TV journalism's great figures, cited the prizes won by the program and added, "The strong remedial action that Congress applied to the problem in the pensions-reform law of 1974 could be NBC's most enduring prize."

"Paul Jacobs and the Nuclear Gang" was broadcast on public television on February 25, 1979. Crusading reporter Jacobs risked his life to tell the story of the high rate of cancer among workers in atomic plants and the people living nearby. The men and women he interviewed had died by the time of the broadcast, and Jacobs himself eventually died of cancer.

Other documentaries in the 1970s covered American problems like hunger, the plight of migrant workers, the struggle of African Americans for equality, threats to the environment, juvenile justice, organized crime, and the U.S. "epidemic" of murder.

These TV documentaries captured public attention for topics that might otherwise have been downplayed or ignored. They reminded people in power that TV can be a powerful watchdog. Over time, these programs affected the thinking and attitudes of citizens, even when results were not immediately evident from actions taken and laws passed.

When television throws time and money, talent and technology into investigative documentaries, something significant happens. It becomes difficult, if not impossible, for the nationwide audience to close its eyes to what's happening in the real world. Rather than an escape, television becomes an eye-opening experience.

PART 4 THE 1980s

18

THE 1980s:

" IF IT WASN'T ON TV, IT WASN'T REAL "

"**D**id the 1980s really even happen?" asked Brian Duffy in an essay in the newsmagazine *U.S. News & World Report* at the end of the decade. Then he answered his own question. "Yes. On television. In a decade when the world's most powerful man was an actor, the planet seemed finally to conclude that if it wasn't on TV, it wasn't real."

In a time of images, the grandest image of all belonged to Ronald Reagan, the former movie actor who was in the White House from 1981 until 1989. He was cheerful, charming, upbeat, and a master of the TV medium.

The president's inner circle programmed his public life in terms of one- or two-minute spots on the evening news. They approached "every presidential appearance in terms of camera angles," according to his close adviser, Donald T. Regan. The president was presented to the nation "as a sort of supreme anchorman."

Reagan proclaimed that America's "optimism has once again been turned loose." His critics would complain that the optimism suffered from a lack of realism. The White House staff countered by selling the image of Reagan, whose popularity overcame the doubters as his landslide reelection demonstrated in 1984. Reagan's eight years in office saw the longest peacetime economic expansion, and also the largest peacetime military buildup, in U.S. history.

But the Republican administration had its problems, too. Many felt that the government was ignoring the country's real problems of poverty and homelessness, decay in its cities, and decline in education. The United States, once the world's leading creditor nation, had become the world's greatest debtor nation—a country living, like many of its citizens, beyond its means. Historian Paul Kennedy of Yale University summed up the Reagan years as "short-term charm and long-term harm."

The 1980s were labeled a decade of greed, when owning, buying, having, and consuming preoccupied Americans. One commercial caught the national mood by promising, "You can have it all." TV advertisers targeted *yuppies* (young urban professionals) as the big spenders. Between 1980 and 1990, TV advertising increased two and a half times to $26.3 billion annually.

Television's biggest success story of the decade featured R. E. "Ted" Turner, who in 1980 launched a twenty-four-hour news operation, the Cable News Network (CNN). Critics said he wouldn't succeed. CNN began operations in the basement of a converted country club with an audience of only 1.7 million U.S. households.

The pessimists were dead wrong. By the early 1990s, CNN's audience encompassed 75 million homes in more than 130 countries and territories. Its staff grew from 300 to 1,700, and profits in 1990 reached $134 million. As commentator Duffy noted, CNN was delivering "all the news, all the exhausting time. And what images!"

Technology was on CNN's side. During the 1980s, satellites led to a boom in cable TV's audience, which grew from 20 percent of U.S. households in 1980 to 56 percent in 1990. By the end of the decade, there were 52 million subscribers. Cable operators offered at least thirty channels, and the industry talked of one hundred in the near future.

Television viewing habits changed radically. Three-fourths of U.S. TV households acquired remote-control devices that allowed viewers to jump from channel to channel and even to watch several programs at the same time. This channel skipping became known as "surfing."

TV news became bigger business than ever, and global coverage was no longer a monopoly of the big three networks, CBS, NBC, and ABC. Satellite news gathering (SNG) came to the fore in the mid-1980s. "CNN LIVE" was flashed on the screen to identify instant coverage anywhere in the world. Local TV news operations got into the act with SNG vans of their own.

Satellites instantly distributed programs anytime, anywhere. An uplink could send a signal to a satellite, which then transmitted the signal to a receiving dish, or downlink. The dish fed the signal to a cable operator or newsroom.

Cable TV's boom came in a decade when money

talked—very loudly—and in a decade of the big business deal—the bigger the better. Business terms like *takeover, leveraged buyout,* and *merger* became as familiar as *home run, touchdown,* and *slam dunk.* The number one show on television, *Dallas,* captured the spirit of the 1980s. Every Friday evening millions watched the saga of greed and cutthroat behavior in the incredibly wealthy fictional Texas family of J. R. Ewing. Among the popular game shows, *Wheel of Fortune* stood out as a show for the 1980s.

For daytime escapism, 80 million viewers a week were watching the romance and intrigue of soap operas. While 80 percent were women between eighteen and forty-nine, the appeal of soap operas spread to include male students and older men. Teenagers went wild over music television (MTV), which started in 1981 and won an audience of 24 million in three years by mixing music with stunning visual effects. The music video was born.

Viewers rushed to buy videocassette recorders (VCRs) to record and play back their favorite programs and to play tapes they bought or rented. VCR sales went from 2 million in 1982 to 12 million in 1985. By the end of the decade, 68 percent of U.S. households owned a VCR and Americans were renting 2 billion tapes a year—from movies to exercise programs to lessons on topics ranging from cooking to making money.

In the 1980s, television doted on a president who left office in 1989 with the highest approval rating of any departing president in more than forty years. "Ronald Reagan enjoyed the most generous treatment by the press of any President in the postwar era,"

Michael Deaver, his deputy chief of staff, stated. "He knew it, and liked the distinction."

Veteran Washington journalist Haynes Johnson summarized a match made in Hollywood: "In the eighties Ronald Reagan and television fitted into American society like a plug into a socket. . . . Americans, with Reagan leading them, were in no mood for being bothered by problems. Reagan, and television, gave them what they most wanted: a chance to feel good again."

19

1980s CONFRONTATION:

" THE SOLDIERS WEREN'T GOING TO COME IN WHILE YOU WERE WATCHING "

THE TIANANMEN SQUARE MASSACRE

Shortly before noon on a Sunday in the spring of 1989, a young man stood in the middle of the Avenue of Eternal Peace in Communist China's capital, Beijing. Alone, he faced a column of twenty-three tanks.

Pro-democracy demonstrators had fled as the tanks moved down the avenue—except for one man wearing a white shirt and dark pants. He did not move as the lead tank came toward him.

CNN Cameraman Jonathan M. Schaer, who was videotaping the episode, expected the worst. "Everyone thought the tank was going to run right over him or shoot him."

Suddenly, the tank stopped six feet in front of the man. He jumped onto its front deck and began pounding on the gun turret. Witnesses heard him shout, "Why are you here? You have done nothing but create misery. My city is in chaos because of you."

Then the man climbed down and stood in front of the tank. When it moved to the right to get around

him, he jumped in front of it. People watching from the side-walk shouted and applauded. The tank tried to get around him again, and again he blocked its way.

Finally, four of his friends led him away down a side street, leaving behind the televised image of one un-armed man standing against the military power of the Communist Chinese government—an oligarchy that ruled more than 1 billion people.

President George Bush reacted along with the worldwide audience. "All I can say to him, wherever he might be, or to people around the world, is: we are and we must stand with him."

For student demonstrators in China—as for those in the United States during the 1960s and 1970s—televi-sion provided the chance to be seen and heard.

A historic summit meeting was taking place be-tween the two giant powers of the Communist world, China and the Soviet Union. It was the first such sum-mit in thirty-one years, and China's leaders had invited the world press. Live U.S. television coverage by CBS and CNN was on hand for the May 15, 1989, visit by Soviet leader Mikhail Gorbachev.

Chinese students and workers seized the opportu-nity to call worldwide attention to pro-democracy demonstrations that had been going on for almost seven weeks. They held a hunger strike in Tiananmen Square, where the TV cameras were set up to cover the Sino-Soviet summit. Soon more than a million Chinese joined the demonstrations.

CNN anchor Bernard Shaw told his audience, "Un-believably, we all came here to cover a summit and we walked into a revolution." CBS anchor Dan Rather commented, "So often our cameras are accused, and rightly so, of distorting an event and making it seem larger than it really is. This time, it seems to me, our cameras are not large enough to take in the scope and importance of this story."

CNN set up its special "flyaway dish" in a Chinese garden behind the Great Wall Sheraton Hotel. The hundred-pound "flyaway" fit into a suitcase and came along as luggage on a passenger jet. It was an uplink to a satellite transponder for immediate connection with CNN's headquarters in Atlanta, Georgia.

Live CNN and CBS coverage showed the hundreds of thousands of people occupying hundred-acre Tiananmen Square in the largest demonstration in modern Chinese history. Live cameras were their allies in holding back the Chinese army hovering around the square.

This was reflected in a touching exchange at CNN's headquarters in a Beijing Hotel. An informal delegation of hotel employees thanked the journalists by telling them, "The soldiers weren't going to come in while you were watching."

"From the beginning, the uprising was a battle of images," *Newsweek* magazine reported. "The students played carefully to the world's TV cameras."

Even their signs were written in English for the sake of the cameras. One sign said, "Be televised live to people," followed by Chinese characters. Another said, "We trust Mr. Democracy." The students even erected a thirty-foot replica of the Statue of Liberty. It was made of Styrofoam covered with plaster and labeled the "Goddess of Democracy."

Finally, an embarrassed Chinese government pulled the plug on satellite transmission. In the closing seconds of CNN's final live broadcast, reporter Steve Hurst

pointed to the "flyaway dish" for worldwide live transmission. Hurst was in awe "that such a small piece of equipment did so much and showed the world so many pictures, so many images so quickly."

Live transmission from Beijing ended on May 20, was restored briefly, and then shut down completely on May 24. After live transmission was stopped, TV journalists reported on the protests over telephone lines and by shipping videotapes to Hong Kong for satellite transmission to the United States. That's how they covered the massacre of Sunday, June 4, 1989, and the subsequent confrontation between man and tank.

Beginning at 2 A.M., ten thousand Chinese troops and tanks unleashed a no-holds-barred attack on the demonstrators in Tiananmen Square. By 5 A.M., the square was empty, the "Goddess of Democracy" demolished, and the hospitals filled with the army's victims. At least a thousand were killed and thousands more wounded.

The world was outraged. The *Wall Street Journal* reported that foreign business leaders were "shocked by the graphic television pictures." Several countries imposed economic sanctions upon China. Investments and transfers of technology worth billions of dollars were put on hold. The heavy flow of tourists to China stopped. The Chinese economy was shaken.

In the United States, the TV coverage shattered the "liberalizing" image that China's leaders had cultivated. There were demonstrations and demands to curtail relations with China. President Bush suspended arms sales and the exchange of military delegations, but he held back from "a total break."

Instead, he warned China that "we can't have totally normal relations unless there's a recognition of the validity of the students' aspirations." As *New York Times* TV columnist Walter Goodman reported, "Television had made heroes of the youths."

"If TV's presence doesn't actually aid democracy," *Newsweek*'s media analyst Jonathan Alter noted, "it may make the cruelest of repressions harder to inflict. Eventually, the whole world will see. Even in China, long oblivious to outside opinions, that makes some difference."

TV's China coverage had particular impact halfway around the world in East Germany, where the citizenry was also restless under a Communist dictatorship. TV producer Tara Sonenshine described in the *Washington Post* an eager audience of East Germans. For them, she reported, television was "a window through which they could witness the revolutionary changes" taking place. It enabled them "to take part in the broad movement to unseat communism around the world." A clergyman told her that East Germans were afraid as they watched televised scenes from Tiananmen Square, but "they were also filled with hope."

Television had also shown East Germans the prosperity of the West Germans next door. The two Germanys had gone their separate ways since the country was divided in 1949 after its defeat in World War II. Although what had been all Germany's capital, Berlin, was located within East Germany, it was divided into Communist East Berlin and democratic West Berlin.

Communist East Germany had always had trouble keeping its people at home. They wanted to leave for

freer and more prosperous lives in West Germany. The rush to defect became so intense that in 1961 the East Germans built the notorious Berlin Wall, which separated East and West Berlin. *Newsweek* magazine described the wall as "a 28-mile-long scar through the heart of a once proud European capital, not to mention the soul of a people."

In the 1980s, with civil unrest and economic depression spreading throughout the Communist-controlled countries of Eastern Europe, the East German government had to make concessions. The most dramatic came at midnight on November 9, 1989, when East Germans won the freedom to travel to West Berlin—a prelude to German reunification the following October.

The Berlin Wall came tumbling down that November night. It was the end of the infamous symbol of the cold war between the Soviet Union and the United States, between communism and free enterprise. East and West Berliners danced together on top of the wall, sang, tooted trumpets, and toasted freedom. They chipped off blocks of concrete from the wall and waved them triumphantly before the cameras. Via satellite, the world joined in celebrating the historic turning point.

"It's not too much of an exaggeration to say that the German revolution began in Tiananmen Square," commented TV producer Sonenshine. She pointed to a final irony: "In China, where some of the impetus for revolutions in East Europe originated, citizens have not been able to see the results. The Chinese leadership . . . understands fully the impact of television. The dramatic images of the crumbling of the Berlin Wall were barely seen in the homes of ordinary Chinese citizens."

Viewers experienced the added wallop of live coverage. TV had already demonstrated the great power of seeing what happened. While seeing goes straight to the emotions uninterrupted, live coverage goes further. It's immediate. It brings viewers to the scene of action so that they feel personally involved as eyewitnesses.

The 1969 moon landing was a preview of what became standard TV fare in the late 1980s. Viewers no longer had to wait to see what had happened. They saw what was happening while it was happening. Americans shared a "you are there" experience as part of the global village.

20

1980s POLITICS:

" AN EMOTIONAL ROLLER COASTER "

THE IRAN HOSTAGE CRISIS

Twenty-eight minutes after Ronald Reagan was sworn in as president on January 20, 1981, a fourteen-month ordeal ended for the United States. Fifty-two U.S. diplomats and embassy employees were freed—they were flying home after 444 excruciating days as hostages in Iran.

CNN split the television screen to cover two events that belonged together not only because they were happening simultaneously, but also because there was a political link. Saturation TV coverage of the hostages had helped elect Reagan.

If Iran had released the hostages before election day the previous November, President Jimmy Carter would have had a surge in popularity that might have added enough votes to edge out Reagan.

Newsweek reported, "America rode an emotional roller coaster of giddy hopes and agonizing disappointments" as Americans watched daily television reports on the hostage crisis for more than a year. Vice President

Former Iranian hostages watch a concert given in their honor from a balcony of the Wiesbaden Airbase hospital in West Germany, January, 1981. (Official U.S. Air Force photo by Johnson Babela: Department of Defense)

Walter Mondale described the pressure of TV coverage upon the president as "tremendous."

The shah of Iran had been a close U.S. ally who ran a repressive and increasingly unpopular regime. In 1979, the Iranian people drove the ailing shah into exile, and Ayatollah Ruhollah Khomeini became supreme religious and political leader. He turned Iran away from the shah's program of Westernization toward Islamic fundamentalism and denounced the United States as "the Great Satan."

The United States opened its doors to the exiled shah for medical treatment in New York City, and on November 4, 1979, Iranian militants attacked the embassy in Tehran and took ninety people, sixty-three of them Americans, hostage. All but fifty-two Americans were released unharmed. The terrorists demanded the return of the shah to Iran in exchange for the remaining hostages.

During the first six months of captivity, the networks devoted about one-third of the nightly news to the hostages. ABC even created a special nightly thirty-minute program, *The Crisis in Iran: America Held Hostage*. The coverage was made more dramatic by interviews with the hostages' families.

The mobs around the embassy in Tehran were choreographed for the cameras. They shouted, chanted, waved their fists, and then quieted when the cameras were turned off. The nightly news showed militants at the embassy where the Americans were held hostage shouting "Kill Carter!" "Kill Americans!" "Kill them all!" They paraded blindfolded hostages before the cameras, and they added insult to injury by burning the American flag.

The hostages became an American obsession, described as "a virtual fixation for the nation" and "a prolonged national nightmare." Beginning in January 1980, the most-watched anchor in television, Walter Cronkite, closed the *CBS Evening News* by counting the days. He signed off by saying: "And that's the way it is on———, the ——th day of the hostages' captivity." Cronkite's influence was so great that *New York Times* columnist James Reston remarked—in a grim joke—that President Carter was acting "as much in response to the 'Ayatollah' Cronkite as to the Ayatollah Khomeini."

President Carter finally responded to pressures to use force. On April 24, 1980, eight helicopters took off from the aircraft carrier *Nimitz* in the Arabian Sea to attempt a rescue by raiding the embassy. Three of the copters broke down en route. When the other copters landed in the Iranian desert to refuel in the dark of night, disaster struck. A refueling aircraft burst into flames, killing eight crew members and wounding five others. Journalist-historian Theodore H. White notes that the success of the raid depended on "maximum surprise, maximum efficiency, maximum luck." The raid had none of these and failed miserably.

Carter went on television to take full responsibility for the attempt and for calling it off "when problems developed." TV viewers had new images and a new threat: the wreckage of U.S. helicopters in the Iranian desert, and Khomeini's threat to kill the hostages if Carter tried another "silly maneuver."

Carter already had enough political trouble at home. Prices were high, and so was unemployment. His relations with Congress and the members of his own Democratic Party were cool, if not unfriendly. He had even had to fight to win renomination in 1980.

In spite of his political problems at home, Carter was running a close race for reelection against Reagan—until the hostage story took another turn just before election day and further weakened his leadership image. By that time, the ailing shah had died in Cairo at age sixty, and Khomeini offered new terms for freeing the hostages.

Carter's campaign manager, Hamilton Jordan, summed up the stakes as the presidential campaign wound down: "If something dramatic happened . . . like the release of the hostages—it would probably allow us to nose Reagan out; a bad signal . . . would probably mean Reagan's election."

Khomeini's new terms were unacceptable and meant no hostage freedom before election day. Once again, American hopes were dashed and on top of that, the first anniversary of the hostage taking was the weekend before the election. Television likes nothing better than to mark anniversaries with special reports. So all the networks closed the nightly news with what Democratic presidential campaign manager Jordan summarized as "an emotionally wrenching review of the past year" in Iran.

Carter's political aides wrung their hands. His press aide, Ray Jenkins, called the anniversary shows "a calamity" for the Carter campaign. Carter's pollster, Pat Caddell, looked at his last preelection poll of voters and concluded, "The sky has fallen in. We are getting murdered. All the people that have been waiting and holding out for some reason to vote Democratic have left us. I've never seen anything like it in polling. Here we are neck and neck with Reagan and everything breaks against us. It's the hostage thing." What had been a close race became a decisive victory for Reagan, setting the stage for the final act in the hostage drama.

Behind the scenes, the United States and Iran had negotiated a deal to free $8 million in frozen Iranian assets in exchange for the hostages. The comment of Iran's negotiator, Behzad Nabavi, was cold-blooded: "The hostages are like a fruit from which all the juice has been squeezed out. Let us let them all go."

The release was orchestrated to coincide with Reagan's inauguration. TV went all out. Satellite hookups shifted from Washington to Algiers (where the hostages' plane stopped) to West Germany (where the hostages were taken for debriefing). Nearly a thousand journalists were on hand in Germany. ABC, CBS, and NBC each had mobilized some four hundred reporters, producers, and technicians to cover the inauguration and the hostage stories. Throughout the United States, local TV anchors interviewed the families of the hostages.

The hostages were welcomed home by their families and by cheering crowds, with motorcades and parades from New York to San Diego, including a special White House ceremony. *Newsweek* reported that "the coast-to-coast celebration was an outpouring of innocent joy." America got a happy ending, and the Reagan administration got off to a great start.

A spontaneous remark by Dan Rather of CBS captured the climax of a story that TV had never left alone. At one point, his voice broke with emotion. "The fifty-two American hostages! All of 'em back!"

But not soon enough for those who ran Carter's reelection campaign.

21

1980s WAR:

" YOU CAN'T COVER A STORY UNLESS YOU'RE THERE !

THE GRENADA INVASION:

OPERATION URGENT FURY

ABC-TV correspondent Steve Shepard was heading for the island country of Grenada, which the United States had just invaded on October 25, 1983. He was bouncing around in a chartered thirty-five-foot boat amid fifteen-foot Caribbean seas when suddenly a U.S. Navy jet swooped in.

Shepard and ABC producer Tim Ross were startled when the jet waggled its wings, passed menacingly overhead, then opened its bomb doors. The U.S. Navy jet pilot was treating him like the enemy.

"The pilot dropped a buoy about thirty feet ahead of us just to show what else he could drop and how close he could drop it," Shepard reported.

Another Grenada-bound fishing boat, chartered by ABC correspondent Josh Mankiewicz, was confronted by a U.S. Navy destroyer. "I got a good look at that gun on the foredeck and decided that we were simply out-classed," he reported.

Image taken from CNN videotape of American soldiers in Grenada, October 1983. (Copyright © 1983 by Cable News Network, Inc. All Rights Reserved)

Both TV correspondents turned around and headed back to Barbados, where they had begun their 160-mile trip to the scene of the invasion.

The U.S. military was warning the press away from the action in no uncertain terms. "I'm down here to take an island," Vice Admiral Joseph Metcalf told protesting reporters. "I don't need you running around and getting in the way. . . . We'll stop you. We've got the means to do that."

Operation Urgent Fury, as the invasion was called, turned out to be short, straightforward, and immediately successful. U.S. forces overwhelmed Grenada's small army and the six hundred Cubans supporting them.

The U.S. government fulfilled the mission it had announced: to protect one thousand Americans in Grenada, including six hundred students at St. George's University School of Medicine. When the students were evacuated and returned home, they provided the U.S. government and the military with the kind of footage they wanted. Grateful evacuees kissed the ground.

U.S. forces overwhelmed pro-Communist rebels who had ousted and executed Grenada's prime minister, Maurice Bishop. Their defeat deprived the Soviet Union of another toehold in the Caribbean (in addition to Cuba).

Although six Caribbean countries had asked for U.S. action and supplied a token force of four hundred, many countries denounced the mission as a violation of international law. For their part, Grenadians welcomed the invaders as liberators.

By the time the military lifted its ban on the press

in Grenada, the Tuesday-to-Thursday invasion was over. Even when let ashore, the reporters were under tight restrictions and could not move freely. Because the military kept correspondents away from the action, TV had no live coverage and was reduced to stock film of Grenada, electronic graphics, and innumerable maps.

Columnist Russell Baker of the *New York Times* concocted a satirical scene that reflected the attitude of President Reagan, the military, and many Americans toward journalists.

In an imaginary pre-invasion briefing, a Pentagon official was addressing a group of officers. He told them he was going "to humiliate one of the most arrogant powers in the world today."

But he didn't mean Grenada's insignificant army or its Communist supporters.

"I *do* mean the American press," he said.

The army colonels and navy captains who fought in Vietnam had become the generals and admirals running the Pentagon during the Grenada invasion. They felt press coverage, particularly TV, had obstructed prosecution of the Vietnam War. They were determined to control the press so it wouldn't happen again in Grenada.

The press protested but did not get public support. Letters to NBC on the issue favored the restrictions ten to one. The other networks and newspapers reported similar responses.

The U.S. military had learned its lesson well. They successfully controlled coverage again six years later in Operation Just Cause: the invasion of Panama.

As in Grenada, the president (this time George

Bush) justified the December 20, 1989, invasion by announcing that he was protecting thirty-five thousand Americans who were in "grave danger." He also wanted to bring to trial Panama's notorious dictator, General Manuel Noriega, who was heavily implicated in international drug dealing.

The invasion involved twenty-four thousand U.S. troops already stationed at the Panama Canal and an additional seven thousand dispatched in the biggest airlift since Vietnam. To the surprise of the U.S. military, they could not deliver an immediate knockout. Resistance collapsed only when Noriega took refuge in the Vatican Embassy, four days after the invasion. He held out for several days before surrendering to be tried in Miami for drug trafficking.

In Grenada and Panama, the U.S. military disarmed TV by keeping cameras away from the action. This broke with a long history of battlefield correspondents covering U.S. wars. More than a hundred went along in the monumental World War II invasion of Normandy, but none in Grenada and Panama.

A frustrated NBC correspondent in Grenada, Richard Valeriani, summed up TV's plight: "We couldn't cover the story. You can't cover a story unless you're there. All we could cover was what we were being told about the story."

After the Grenada blackout, the American Society of Newspaper Editors protested to the government: "We object to the Defense Department's failure to honor the long tradition of on-the-scene coverage of military operations."

But television had changed the nature of media coverage, first in Korea and much more so in Vietnam.

Emotionally charged live-action scenes, including the sight of Americans being wounded and killed, brought home the price of war as no newspaper article could.

The military acted in what it regarded as self-defense against painful images that could threaten public support.

22

1980s HEROES AND VILLAINS:

" WE ALL SHARED IN THIS EXPERIENCE "

CHRISTA McAULIFFE

*A*ll day long on Tuesday, January 28, 1986, Americans watched the same videotape replayed at regular speed, in slow motion, and in stop action.

At 11:38 A.M., the space shuttle *Challenger* rose majestically into a clear, blue sky above the Atlantic Ocean off the east coast of Florida. This was its tenth flight and the fifty-sixth U.S. manned mission in space.

The seven on board were a slice of America—male, female, African-American, Asian-American, white, Catholic, Jewish, Protestant. They were mission commander Francis R. Scobee; astronauts Michael J. Smith, Ronald E. McNair, Ellison Onizuka, Judith A. Resnik, and Gregory B. Jarvis; and the first passenger chosen to go into space, Sharon Christa McAuliffe.

The public-address system announced the countdown at Cape Canaveral: "Four . . . three . . . two . . . one . . . and liftoff. Liftoff of the twenty-fifth space shuttle mission. And it has cleared the tower." Onlookers cheered.

At thirty-five seconds into the flight, the space shut-

Official portrait of Payload Specialist Sharon Christa McAuliffe, Teacher in Space, Citizen Observer of the space shuttle *Challenger*, taken September 20, 1985. (Courtesy of NASA)

tle was traveling 1,538 miles per hour, its three engines running normally at 65 percent of full power.

At fifty-two seconds, the engines reached full power. Mission Control in Houston radioed to Commander Scobee: "*Challenger,* go with throttle up."

Scobee replied: "Roger, go with throttle up."

At 11:39:13 A.M., the spaceship was traveling 1,977 miles an hour, ten miles up and eight miles downrange. Seventy-three seconds into flight, the $1.2 billion space shuttle burst into flame. The 154-foot-high external tank ignited. Its 143,351 gallons of liquid oxygen and 385,265 gallons of liquid hydrogen exploded, raining down hundreds of melted fragments.

Time writer Lance Morrow described the sight: "A sudden burst of white and yellow fire, then white trails streaming up and out from the fireball to form a twisted Y against a pure heaven and the metal turning to rags, dragging white ribbons into the ocean."

The contrast was chilling. One moment excitement and cheers, the next shock and tears. The president's wife, Nancy Reagan, who was in the White House watching the launch, said what people say when they don't want to believe what they see: "Oh, my God, no!" Tom Mintier, CNN's narrator, was shocked into silence for several seconds. For more than five hours, the networks canceled all programs and commercials to concentrate on the disaster. In the evening, each network broadcast an hour-long special in prime time. Throughout the coverage, TV kept coming back to the videotape of *Challenger*'s final seconds. Repeated showings of the disaster made it hit even harder, burning "the sickening fireball into our brains" (as the *New York Times* editorialized).

More than eight hundred journalists were on hand at the Kennedy Space Center on Cape Canaveral for the liftoff, five times as many as for the previous shuttle flight. The 2,500 guests included husbands, wives, children, parents, and friends of the *Challenger* seven.

The center of attention was thirty-seven-year-old Christa McAuliffe, a schoolteacher who had become a national celebrity after being chosen from eleven thousand applicants to be a passenger.

She was an ideal choice: devoted wife, mother of nine-year-old Scott and six-year-old Caroline, dedicated high school social-science teacher, and a space enthusiast who was "rarin' to go." Well-spoken, likable, photogenic, she became a favorite on TV news and talk shows.

Christa explained why she wanted to be on board: "What are we doing here? We're reaching for the stars." She also had a sense of mission as a teacher. "I touch the future. I teach." After her space trip, she was going right back to her students.

Time called her "our representative in space. . . . She called herself 'an ordinary person,' and that is how many fellow citizens, stirred and flattered by what she was attempting on their behalf, came to think of her."

For U.S. children, it was the first national tragedy that included them specifically. NASA had set up a much-publicized "teacher in space" program. On launch day, teachers turned on classroom TVs to watch with their students. Once in space, Christa McAuliffe was going to teach two fifteen-minute lessons to millions of schoolchildren via closed-circuit TV. They took the disaster personally, experiencing what *U.S. News & World Report* called "a lesson in grief for the young."

Some had nightmares, all needed explanations of what happened.

Space travel didn't lose its appeal despite the tragic reminder of its risks. Polls showed that most Americans still supported manned space flights and wanted the government to keep funding them. But NASA paid a price as a government agency. The media, which had glamorized the space agency, began criticizing the way NASA operated. Shuttle missions went on indefinite hold. A special presidential commission blamed the disaster on mismanagement at the space agency and bad decision making at the time of the launch. The explosion that destroyed the *Challenger* was traced to a rupture in a faulty O-ring seal on a booster rocket that let a jet of flame escape and ignited the fuel.

On the evening of the explosion, President Reagan set aside his State of the Union message to televise a heartwarming tribute to the *Challenger* "heroes . . . daring and brave . . . they served all of us." It was Reagan at his best, a leader who expressed the nation's feelings.

He included a message to the schoolchildren of America who had watched the takeoff and explosion: "I know it's hard to understand that sometimes painful things like this happen. . . . It's all part of taking a chance and expanding man's horizons. The future doesn't belong to the faint-hearted. It belongs to the brave. The *Challenger* crew was pulling us into the future and we'll continue to follow them."

He also emphasized that the cameras would always be on hand. "We don't hide our space program, we don't keep secrets and cover things up. That's the way freedom is and we wouldn't change it for a minute."

In so many words, Reagan faced up to the risk of

letting the cameras watch. TV made the nation care about its *Challenger* heroes and then brought millions face-to-face with their tragedy. Such moments had become part of the American experience—part of growing up and living in America.

ABC anchor Peter Jennings sounded a familiar refrain in the age of live coverage: "We all shared in this experience in an instantaneous way because of television."

23

1980s EYE-OPENERS:

THE POWER TO " GALVANIZE THE U.S. PUBLIC "

FAMINE IN ETHIOPIA

In war- and drought-plagued Ethiopia, thousands of starving refugees sat or lay in the sand, too weak to move. Swarms of flies covered the eyes and mouths of listless children who didn't have the strength to brush them away.

In New York, when anchor Tom Brokaw and the staff of *NBC Nightly News* previewed these scenes, the newsroom was "brought to a complete silence," recalled executive producer Paul Greenberg. "Tears came to your eyes and you felt as if you'd just been hit in the stomach."

The evening of October 23, 1984, millions of viewers had the same reaction when the news program concluded with the famine scenes. They responded with phone calls, letters, donations, and offers to volunteer to go to Ethiopia to help.

Members of Congress demanded governmental action. TV coverage stimulated millions of dollars in donations and prompted increased U.S. government aid for Ethiopia.

As *Newsweek* reported: "The surge of sympathy and aid was dramatic testimony to the impact of television."

Up to that point, many newspaper articles had appeared with little or no impact. *Washington Post* writer Joanne Omamg called the reaction of the TV audience "a lesson in the relatively feeble power of anything but television to galvanize the U.S. public." Once again, TV demonstrated how the impact of viewing surpasses reading or hearing about something.

Seeing the victims was an overpowering experience. Americans felt a sense of responsibility. One mother's note accompanying a hundred-dollar donation to a relief agency in Boston read: "I think of Ethiopia every time I look at my fat happy baby."

Exactly four years later in October 1988, Tom Brokaw closed the *NBC Nightly News* with a very different TV report that also stirred nationwide sympathy. The setting was in frigid Point Barrow, Alaska, the northernmost spot in the United States. This time, the focus was on three endangered whales.

It only became a big story because the cameras were there. A TV reporter read a story about the whales in the local Anchorage, Alaska, newspaper and went to the scene to film them. Via satellite, the footage was sent to a Seattle NBC affiliate and then transmitted to New York for the *NBC Nightly News.*

For three weeks thereafter, TV was dominated by efforts to free the whales. Trapped in an ice-filled inlet and unable to reach the open seas, they were in danger of being caught beneath the ice. Because whales are mammals, if they were unable to come up for air, they would suffocate.

"Once the whales entered America's living rooms,

they became, in effect, giant pets," *Time* magazine reported.

They were given names: Bonnet, Crossbeak, and Bone. President Reagan telephoned rescue workers to tell them that "our hearts are with you and our prayers are also with you."

Rescuing the whales became an ongoing suspense-filled drama. At one point, 150 journalists from four continents converged on the site. At least twenty-six TV networks from all over the world were represented. The coverage cost about $26 million.

TV went all out to satisfy the audience interest it had created. The networks "could not get enough" footage of the rescue effort, journalist Tom Rose stated in *Freeing the Whales*, a book-length study of the coverage.

"The better the video, the more of it the networks aired," he reported. "The more they aired, the more enthralled the public became. The more enthralled the public became, the more pressure was put on the rescuers to save the whales. Almost as fast as the story broke, the rescue was controlled by a force beyond anyone's control, the force of collective human fascination."

When one of the whales drowned, the world mourned. When the Soviet Union sent two icebreakers, which ultimately freed the remaining two whales, the world cheered.

Before the TV-induced "Operation Rescue" rescue was over, several helicopters, support vehicles, and more than one hundred people were involved. Marine biologists were amazed at the gigantic effort to save three whales, since whales often become trapped. In fact, thirty miles from the rescue site polar bears were feasting on a whale that had died while trapped, unnoticed by the media.

All that money, time, and resources were spent on three whales while projects to save entire species of whales went begging. *Time* magazine raised a key point: "How can the human outpouring of concern for three whales, however sentimental or misplaced, be translated into real protection for whales in general?"

As different as the Alaska and Ethiopian stories were, they illustrated basic truths about television and its audience: Both stories showed—once again—how statistics about starvation could leave the audience cold, but faces of starving men, women, and children are overwhelming. Reports about endangered animal species are abstract. But close-ups of three specific whales gasping for breath at Arctic ice holes pulls at heartstrings, particularly when the audience has made them into "giant pets."

Once the public was aroused, TV networks and stations went all out to satisfy its interest. A feeding frenzy took over and this, in turn, increased the public's appetite. What the audience wanted TV supplied in order to win the largest possible audience. That's how stations and networks succeed (and survive).

To appeal to the audience on an ongoing basis, TV must choose from a flood of events, issues, and crises, leaving out much more than it reports. And TV has learned that the relative importance of an event is no guarantee of audience interest.

For example in 1988, the year of "Operation Rescue," Ethiopia had another terrible famine. Television covered it extensively, but there was no powerful public reaction. People had seen it all four years before. Instead, the audience became absorbed in the fate of three trapped whales in Alaska.

One relief official, Laura Kullenberg of Oxfam in Boston cited her experience: "the media's and the public's attention spans are very short."

After the media-generated surge of contributions for the Ethiopian famine in 1984, relief donations dropped below what they had been before. It has been called "compassion fatigue." People soon get enough of a story, the unceasing bombardment of other news distracts them, and they go on to the next sensation.

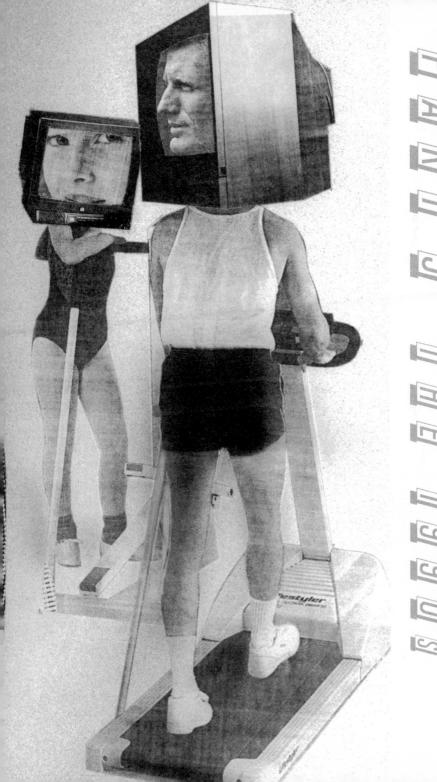

PART 5 THE 1990s

24

THE 1990s:

" THE PARTY WAS OVER "

The new decade was only a year old when *Newsweek* magazine announced that "the party was over . . . [the 1990s are] clearly shaping up as a far more turbulent—and anxious—age than the eighties."

President Reagan had proclaimed that it was "Morning in America." This was replaced by a morning-after mood, a gloomy hangover. In 1988, 50 percent of Americans thought the country was on the wrong track. By 1990, the percentage of pessimists reached 80 percent.

The country's worries were personal and practical. They centered on the "good life" that always had been taken for granted. Polls confirmed that the U.S. economy had become the number one concern, jobs in particular. Sixty-three percent of those Americans polled said that someone they knew well was out of work and looking for a job. In early 1993, 40 percent said that the chances were high that an adult family member would be unemployed in the next twelve months.

Americans were no longer taking things for granted. As the decade began, only 26 percent of those polled believed their children would have a better life than they did. More Americans (43 percent) saw Japan as the number one economic power in the next century than saw the United States (39 percent) in that top position.

In the 1990s, television, as always, is giving the public a heavy dosage of information and coverage that mixes the serious and the sensational. The reason is clear. TV depends on attracting an audience for its advertisers and relies on ratings to report on what the audience wants to watch. More than in previous decades, the answer is live coverage of dramatic events, exposure of scandals, investigation of wrongdoing, inside stories about the famous and the powerful, and no-holds-barred airing of sensitive topics. In short, information packaged as entertainment.

By 1990, the three major networks were feeling the competition from cable as well as VCRs. Between 1980 and 1990, the percentage of Americans watching prime-time network shows on a weekday evening dropped from 90 to 60 percent. In that time, the percentage of households with cable TV soared from 20 percent to 56 percent, and it continues to rise.

The networks were responding to public demand by offering "more information in prime time than ever before in the history of the medium," according to *Newsweek* TV analyst Jonathan Alter.

At mid-decade, ten weekly hour-long network news magazines are running in prime time, not including nightly network news and occasional specials. That's about ten times as much as in earlier decades.

Cable TV offers the twenty-four-hour news service of Cable News Network, which includes special reports, special assignment investigative reports, and news features. For those who want to watch Congress, C-SPAN provides live viewing augmented by the most serious public-affairs discussions in all television.

Talk shows are a major part of television's delivery of information on both the networks and cable. Daytime, they are pushing aside soap operas in commanding attention and audience. Late night, they offer an army of hosts who vary from the genial to the outrageous. Overall, talk shows offer topics that know no limits and guests who range from advice-giving experts to zany show-offs.

Cable TV adds to the information explosion with more and more channels devoted to specialized information—from gardening to golf, from business to health. All this is happening as cable looks ahead to an era of five hundred channels.

The O. J. Simpson trial was the epitome of saturation TV coverage. No prime-time series could compare with this real-life drama. O. J. became the media's latest obsession—an obsession that grew throughout his trial. No criminal case has ever received such TV coverage. Yet the way the Simpson story was covered was not unique in the history of television. It was another example of how far TV will go to satisfy its audience.

25

1990s CONFRONTATION:

" THEY JUST DON'T GET IT "

CLARENCE THOMAS AND ANITA HILL

The Judiciary Committee of the U.S. Senate and millions of TV viewers watched law professor Anita Hill and Judge Clarence Thomas contradict each other.

The confrontation was fascinating and also frustrating. Fascinating because Thomas's nomination to the U.S. Supreme Court was at stake, and frustrating because it seemed impossible to decide who was lying.

Hill accused Thomas of having sexually harassed her while she worked for him at the U.S. Department of Education and the Equal Employment Opportunity Commission (EEOC) from 1981 to 1983. If the charges were true, Thomas was not fit for Senate confirmation.

Hill, a thirty-five-year-old professor of law at the University of Oklahoma, was a conscientious, church-going Southern Baptist, a woman described by colleagues as "a good, sincere human being."

Thomas, once a seminarian studying to be a Catholic priest, was a forty-three-year-old judge in a federal court of appeals. The White House produced the

Images taken from CNN videotape of Anita Hill and Clarence Thomas testifying during Senate Judiciary Committee hearings on Judge Thomas's nomination to the U.S. Supreme Court, October 11, 1991. (Copyright © 1991 by Cable New Network, Inc. All Rights Reserved)

names of former Thomas employees who vouched for his character. One of them called Hill's charges "inconceivable."

Hill's charges became public after the fourteen senators on the Judiciary Committee had completed hearings on the Thomas nomination. The committee tied seven to seven on recommending Thomas, so it decided to send his nomination to the full Senate without a recommendation.

Hill had told a friend that Thomas sexually harassed her when he was her boss as EEOC chairman in charge of enforcing federal laws against such harassment. Inevitably, the story leaked out.

The Judiciary Committee couldn't ignore the charges and the subsequent national uproar. So it reopened hearings on Thomas, setting the stage for a televised showdown beginning on Friday, October 11, 1991.

After both made opening statements, Thomas testified first. He vehemently rejected Hill's charges, denying that he had tried to make dates with Hill while she worked for him. He refuted her claims that he had discussed dirty movies with her and that he had boasted about himself in a sexual way.

"I have not said or done the things Anita Hill has alleged," he told the committee. He was indignant. He displayed righteous anger. At times he was nearly in tears. He said that "God has gotten me through . . . and he is my judge."

But Hill was equally convincing as an accuser. During seven hours of testimony, she looked the senators in the eye as she testified about the fear, humiliation, and embarrassment she suffered. She was cool, direct, polite, and emphatic in describing offensive language and behavior. She told the nation: "I felt that I had to tell the truth."

"Hill had given the most lurid description of any man's behavior that had ever been witnessed on network TV," *U.S. News & World Report* stated.

"They are both credible, intelligent, well-educated, both lawyers, both testifying under oath, and one is lying," Vermont Senator Patrick J. Leahy said after listening to them at televised hearings of the Judiciary Committee. "There's no other conclusion I could reach. Which one it is, I don't know."

"She Said, He Said," intoned a *Time* magazine headline: "two credible, articulate witnesses present irreconcilable views of what happened nearly a decade ago."

In the Friday confrontation, Thomas benefited from the strategy used by his Republican supporters on the Judiciary Committee. They made certain that he had the chance to answer Hill's compelling testimony in prime time.

This gave him both the last word and the largest audience. At 9 P.M., 20.8 million Americans saw Thomas denounce what was happening as "a high-tech lynching for uppity blacks." The timing and his emotional presentation helped to build immediate two-to-one support for Thomas in public opinion polls.

Hill's testimony and Thomas's testimony were followed on Saturday and Sunday by those of numerous character witnesses. TV coverage totaled twenty-one hours.

The hearings transfixed the country. Nine out of ten people polled said they had watched at least part of the hearings. Viewers turned away from daytime soap operas and baseball play-offs to watch. At work, they turned on TVs. At home, they changed plans in order to watch the weekend sessions. Viewers shouted at the TV set; wives argued with husbands. More important, women disclosed their own experiences with harassment on the job, and men took a second look at their dealings with women co-workers.

The Thomas-Hill hearings were in the same marbled Senate Caucus Room that had held the Army-McCarthy hearings in 1954 and the Watergate hearings in 1973. Once again, the prestige of the U.S. government was at stake.

Race was also a factor. Both Hill and Thomas were African-American success stories, rising from poor backgrounds to positions of prestige. Many blacks questioned Hill's priorities. Some felt she was putting women's rights ahead of loyalty to African-American advancement. "It's kind of like black people doing each other in," commented Dr. Alvin F. Poussaint, a Harvard University psychiatrist and specialist on racism.

But the overriding issue was how women are treated by men in positions of power. The images on the TV screen put the issue on display. Anita Hill was one woman facing an all-male Judiciary Committee, which represented a U.S. Senate that was all-white and 98 percent male.

Albert A. Gore, who as a senator opposed Thomas's nomination before and after the hearings, underlined the significance of what was going on: "The revolution in thought about relationships between men and women is shaking the Senate and the country." Committee Chairman Joseph R. Biden Jr. called it a "power struggle going on in this country between men and women . . . the biggest thing you can imagine."

Many people were indignant when the senators were slow to grasp the seriousness of Hill's charges. They were outraged at the way she was treated as a witness. Republican members of the committee went all out to protect the man who was accused and to discredit his female accuser.

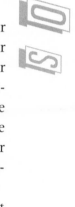

The respected *New York Times* columnist Tom Wicker charged that President George Bush authorized "gutter tactics" against Hill. Wicker complained that "senator after senator repeated mindlessly that he [Thomas] 'deserved the benefit of the doubt.'" They acted as if the hearings were a court of law instead of a way to make sure the nominee was of the highest quality. Wicker commented that the country ended up with "a questionable nominee."

A single complaint summarized women's outrage at the failure of men in power to understand the issue: "They just don't get it." It was heard in protests, speeches, and TV interviews.

Women demonstrated in the streets after the Senate confirmed President Bush's choice of Clarence Thomas as a Supreme Court justice by a vote of fifty-two to forty-eight—the narrowest margin of approval in 103 years. Their signs read: WE WILL REMEMBER . . . NEXT NOVEMBER.

And they did.

"We will no longer beg for our rights from men in power," said Patricia Ireland, executive vice president of the National Organization for Women. "We will replace them and take power ourselves."

A record eleven women ran for the U.S. Senate. Five won including, Carol Moseley Braun, who became the first African-American woman elected to the Senate. She had scored a major upset in the Illinois Democratic primary against Senator Alan Dixon, who had supported Thomas. In the House of Representatives, women won a record forty-six seats.

Political analysts noted that the Republican Party lost support among women after its senators led the attack on Hill. The repercussion won votes for Democratic presidential candidate Bill Clinton. His victorious campaign for president became known as "Anita Hill's revenge."

Whereas women hesitated previously to complain of sexual harassment, things began to change. The Equal Employment Opportunity Commission, once headed by Thomas, reported that harassment complaints doubled in the two years after the hearings.

One year after the hearings, Anita Hill emerged as a folk hero for many Americans, particularly women. Meanwhile, Thomas lost his majority support in public opinion polls.

Right after the hearings, 60 percent had believed Thomas, 20 percent had believed Hill. (Supporters of Hill blamed this on the fact that Thomas testified at the best time to get a large audience and that he had the last word on the witness stand.) A year later, as many Americans believed Hill as believed Thomas—38 percent.

Three years later, Harriett Woods, president of the National Women's Political Caucus, said: "Look where we've come since 1991." At the hearings, "the battle was to have sexual harassment taken seriously. Now sexual harassment seems the most accepted, telling charge you could make against someone in power."

The hearings showed how television had become part of government. Chairman Biden acknowledged this fact when his committee discussed holding a closed meeting on Hill's charges. This was impossible, he said, because "the public would be outraged." The hearings had to be in the open, and that automatically included live coverage.

Television had become part of a well-established political process. Americans tuned in and made up their own minds about important issues. Instead of on-lookers, they became judge and jury. They formed opinions based on what they saw on TV and let politicians, members of Congress, and the White House know what they thought with phone calls, letters, faxes, public opinion polls—and in the voting booth. Once again, TV had demonstrated tremendous power to galvanize American society.

In the wake of the televised Hill-Thomas confrontation, women's demand for equality and fair treatment picked up greater momentum. Women became much more politically active. Men, particularly those in power, had to listen and respond. They began to "get it."

25

1990s POLITICS:

GIVING CANDIDATES
" TO THE AMERICAN PEOPLE DIRECTLY "

THE 1992 PRESIDENTIAL CAMPAIGN

On the road to the White House in 1992, President Bill Clinton helped to write a new chapter in presidential campaigning by doing the following things on television: He played the saxophone on *The Arsenio Hall Show* wearing wraparound dark glasses and a phosphorescent blue-and-yellow tie. He answered viewer phone calls on a CBS "town meeting" and did the same on the NBC morning show, *Today*. He appeared twice on the *Larry King Live* talk show within two weeks, and he chatted with voters having breakfast in a New Jersey diner on ABC's *Good Morning America*.

Clinton, along with the other 1992 presidential candidates, was reaching out to the people live and direct.

The candidates were no longer depending on the network nightly news, on televised panels of reporters, and on presidential debates with set formats to deliver their messages. They took power away from TV anchors with famous faces and columnists with well-

Presidential candidate Bill Clinton playing the saxophone on the *Arsenio Hall Show,* c. June 1992. (Photo by Reed Saxton: AP/Wide World Photos)

known bylines by reaching voters via talk shows, televised town hall meetings, and paid, half-hour "infomercials."

President Bush, as a sitting president, was at first reluctant to appear on talk shows. It was not "presidential." But he had no choice. He had to join in or give an advantage to his opponents. By the time the campaign heated up in October, Bush had appeared on *Larry King Live* twice in one week.

Larry King became the "father of electronic democracy" on February 20, 1992, when Ross Perot, a computer tycoon, made his fourth appearance in thirteen months on King's show. Perot offered to run for president if his supporters organized themselves and put his name on the ballot. There was an immediate nationwide response. Switchboards at newspapers and broadcast stations were jammed with phone calls.

Thanks to a talk show and his straight-talking style, Perot was launched as an independent candidate with groups springing up all over the country to support him. He became a powerful political force that both Democrats and Republicans had to deal with and eventually a factor in Clinton's victory.

The 1992 race for the White House was called a "talk show campaign." It was also called an "electronic town hall" because of candidates' town hall meetings televised in different parts of the country.

The meetings had the added appeal of unpredictability. Candidates had to be ready for surprises. At one televised town hall meeting in Portland, Oregon, a man stood up and asked Clinton live, via satellite: "I am a pagan witch, and I would like to know how you feel about atheism and pagan witchcraft."

TV talk shows with their millions of viewers had a field day featuring political candidates. In exchange the candidates were given a national audience and a free hand to put across their messages and their personalities. Through talk shows, they reached people who otherwise might not pay much attention to politics and politicians.

To extend their reach even further, candidates and their political teams had C-SPAN and MTV, as well as radio talk shows. Network news programs no longer dominated political coverage. One CBS survey found that among people aged eighteen to twenty-nine, 30 percent of those polled said they heard some campaign news for the first time from comedians on late-night TV.

In addition, satellites and cable TV enabled the candidates to bypass the networks and to change their images to appeal to different constituents. The Bush campaign prepared tailor-made speeches and advertisements and sent them by satellite to local stations based on regional demographics. A Republican strategist explained: "Somebody watching TV in Ohio will get a totally different campaign from someone in California."

The Democrats placed speakers on local cable shows to back up what Clinton said in his national speeches. Both parties made a special effort to get coverage on news shows in key voting regions. The growth of news outlets had "made the media much more democratic," noted Clinton media adviser Mandy Grunwald.

The change toward localized, niche-marketed campaigns suited the public. Voters had become suspicious of aloof politicians and weary of platforms that did not reflect their concerns. Many had also turned against the press.

197

Polls reflected this trend. The Gallup Poll reported in 1989 that more than two-thirds of the people said that journalists tend to favor one side. That was up from 53 percent in 1985. Congress's image also was declining. In March 1991, a *Newsweek* poll found that only one out of three Americans had "a great deal" or "quite a lot" of confidence in Congress.

A study by the Freedom Forum Media Studies Center also documented the decline of news commentators in favor of entertainers as opinion makers. In 1988, the most trusted sources of information were TV analysts, print commentators, and political operatives. In 1992, print journalists were practically gone from the list. For the first time, the top ten included three talk show hosts: Larry King, ranked number two; Arsenio Hall, number five; and Phil Donahue, number ten.

The talk shows created a "living room effect." One-time presidential hopeful Gary Hart talked to King about it. "The longer a person is in your living room, the more you can decide for yourself whether he or she makes any sense, is telling the truth, is of sound character, and [has] all the qualities you want for national leadership."

As *Time* magazine commentator Richard Zoglin pointed out, political issues can be "overrated" in a presidential campaign. "An hour or two of spontaneous give-and-take provides an important glimpse of the candidate in real, human interaction: a taste of his temperament, a reading of his sincerity, a feeling for how he relates to people and to pressure."

When the Bush and Clinton campaign teams were setting the ground rules for the three presidential debates, Clinton's side insisted on formatting the second debate as a town meeting. More than two hundred undecided voters had the chance to question Bush, Clinton, and Perot as the nation watched.

The crucial moment for Bush came when a woman asked about the nation's economic problems. The president, more comfortable with formal debates, was having trouble answering. The woman interrupted to ask, "You, on a personal basis, how has it affected you?"

Bush's answer failed to make contact with her concerns. His words sounded cold and formal. He didn't reach out to the woman. At one point, he said of the question, "I'm not sure I get it." The Democrats pounced on his answer, an example of the perils of the "electronic town hall." It may have been the single most damaging episode for the Bush campaign—producing the impression that the president was out of touch with the common people, that he "didn't get it."

It soon became apparent why the Democrats had opted for a town meeting. Clinton was in his element. Unlike Bush, who answered the woman while sitting, Clinton walked to the edge of the stage and talked directly to her. He described what he had seen in his twelve years as "governor of a small state." He described how it "affected" him when people "lost their jobs, lost their livelihood, lost their health insurance."

Clinton showed his mastery of the informal style of talk shows and town meetings. He came across as a candidate with feelings for the average person, a significant plus.

In talk show and town meeting campaigning, the candidates faced individual voters who wanted to know what candidates were like and how they felt about issues.

By contrast, in traditional interviews and press

conferences, reporters' questions reflected their expert knowledge of the latest political developments, charges, and tactics. Their questions were specific, insiders' questions and often of little interest to the general public. Reporters were looking for controversy and headlines. The voters were just trying to make up their minds whom to vote for.

With journalists in charge of the questions, average voters felt like spectators. Talk shows and town hall meetings made them feel like participants. Even though only a few people got the chance to ask questions, viewers felt as if one of them was doing the asking.

Looking back, Larry King described the campaign in a book whose title said it all: *On the Line: The New Road to the White House.* He pinpointed the appeal of talk shows: "the chance to communicate directly, unfiltered by the press."

Clinton was in office only six months when a leading Republican, Jack Kemp, discussed the 1996 presidential campaign on *Larry King Live.* He promised a call-in viewer that if he announced his candidacy in 1996, he would do so on King's talk show!

After his inauguration as the forty-second U.S. president, Clinton discussed what had happened in political campaigning. He had the appropriate audience—the Radio and Television Correspondents' Association—and the right message: "Larry King has liberated me from you by giving me to the American people directly."

27

1990s WAR:

ERASING
" THE STIGMA OF VIETNAM "

THE GULF WAR: OPERATION DESERT STORM

During prime time on January 16, 1991, when U.S. planes bombed Baghdad to begin the Gulf War, Gilbert Lavoie, the Canadian prime minister's press secretary, phoned Marlin Fitzwater, President Bush's press secretary.

"Hi, what are you doing?" Fitzwater asked.

"I'm doing the same thing you are—watching CNN," Lavoie replied.

Worldwide, from government ministries to private homes, sets were tuned to the Cable News Network. In the age of live global coverage, not only did the public turn to TV to find out what was happening. So did those in power.

They watched Operation Desert Storm get under way, a U.S.-led war five months in the making. Iraq had invaded its small, oil-rich neighbor Kuwait on August 2, 1990. One hundred thousand Iraqi troops and three hundred tanks overwhelmed Kuwait's army of sixteen thousand. The excuse for invasion was a dispute over

Image taken from CNN videotape of U.S. soldiers in Saudi Arabia during Operation Desert Storm c. January 1991. (Copyright © 1991 by Cable News Network, Inc. All Rights Reserved)

land and oil, but the goal of the Iraqi dictator, Saddam Hussein, was control of Kuwait's vast oil resources and wealth (including its 100-billion-dollar "Fund for the Future").

The invasion alarmed the world by threatening to reduce the supply and increase the price of oil on which modern economies depended. It also endangered the stability of the governments in the strategically important Middle East. The threat was so great that the United States and the Soviet Union, enemies during the cold war, joined to condemn the invasion. In September 1990, President Bush announced on television that the United States was ready to use force if necessary to drive Iraq out of Kuwait.

A massive buildup of troops, tanks, ships, and air power in the Persian Gulf made his intentions clear. By January 1991, the United States land-sea-air force in the Middle East numbered 527,000.

The United Nations had given Iraq a January 16 deadline to leave Kuwait—or else. The "or else" was authority for a U.S.-led coalition of twenty-eight nations "to use all necessary means" to drive Iraq out of Kuwait.

First came a televised war of words:

From Saddam Hussein: "Should the Americans become embroiled, we will make them swim in their own blood, God willing."

From George Bush: "There are times in life we confront values worth fighting for. This is one such time."

When the January 16 deadline passed without an Iraqi withdrawal, the United States led the coalition into action, launching the first war televised live and broadcast globally. CNN's role was unprecedented.

Never before had a war been reported live by reporters in the enemy's capital. They were on the air as U.S. planes rained down bombs.

In Baghdad, suddenly the city's dogs had started barking wildly. In the next instant, a huge flash lit the southern sky. Peter Arnett of CNN, who would become world famous as the only U.S. correspondent who remained in Baghdad for the first three weeks of the bombing, looked at his watch. It was 2:32 A.M. in Baghdad, eight hours earlier in New York—prime time for television.

Arnett described "tremendous lightning in the sky . . . it looks like the Fourth of July."

"It's like the center of hell," added CNN's John Holliman, who was in a ninth-floor room in Baghdad's Rashid Hotel with Arnett and CNN anchor Bernard Shaw. The three were dubbed CNN's "Boys of Baghdad."

As they began covering the first night's bombing, they heard from the CNN control room in Atlanta: "Go for it guys. The whole world's watching."

Technology made the coverage possible. For live video coverage, CNN had set up a portable "flyaway" video uplink for transmission via satellite. For its live audio coverage on the night of the bombing, CNN had a "four wire" overseas telephone connection, which functioned without telephone operators or switching connections, even without local electric service.

This was CNN's trademark: live global coverage of what was happening while it happened. At the peak of the war, CNN had 150 broadcasters, technicians, and support people in the Gulf area. Worldwide, it had another 1,500 working on the story.

Although the TV picture was lost soon after the first

attacks, CNN's "Boys of Baghdad" continued their audio reports. Seventeen hours later, Baghdad security officials shut them down. All correspondents were ordered to leave Baghdad, except for Arnett. Initially, Arnett used a satellite telephone to broadcast reports from Baghdad. Twelve days after the first attack, a CNN truck arrived from Amman, Jordan, 520 miles away, with a satellite uplink for live TV transmission.

Eventually, as Iraq let Western journalists return, the other U.S. networks and broadcasters from around the world joined CNN in the enemy capital. The world saw the air war not only as it happened in Baghdad, but also in Israel, Kuwait, and Saudi Arabia (which faced attacks by Iraqi Scud missiles because it was part of the U.S.-led coalition).

Tomahawk missiles streaked across the Baghdad skyline, Scud missiles came blazing out of the night sky and shook the ground with explosions. What was on the screen often seemed unreal. "It's like a Nintendo game," a CNN correspondent commented.

It did seem like a game. Even the U.S. bombs raining down on Iraq carried cameras that focused on the targets they were approaching. The images produced by these camera-carrying bombs were passed on to viewers, the ultimate TV report.

But the death, destruction, and danger were real. Live coverage communicated the sense of danger by showing war correspondents in the midst of the action. On camera, TV reporters donned gas masks against the threat of chemical warfare. At various times, they abruptly stopped broadcasting and headed for bomb shelters with their crews.

In one fearful night, live TV showed both Israel and

Saudi Arabia under attack by Iraqi Scud missiles. CNN's Charles Jaco was broadcasting from a coalition air base in Dhahran, Saudi Arabia, when he reported an explosion in his direction.

"Fold it up and go," a voice shouted from the CNN control room in Atlanta.

On screen, Jaco shouted to his TV crew: "Okay, guys. Break it down. Outa here. Let's go."

The screen went blank.

For a few moments, viewers were left in suspense. Then transmission was resumed, showing that the crew was safe.

In another memorable episode, NBC correspondent Arthur Kent broadcast from a roof in Dhahran, microphone in one hand, gas mask in the other. Shouting over the screech of an air-raid siren, he pointed to a streak of light in the sky. A U.S. Patriot missile was racing toward an Iraqi Scud missile. The explosion marked the Patriot's dazzling TV debut.

Throughout the forty-three-day war, TV once again demonstrated its power to command attention, arouse emotions, and create overnight celebrities. When President Bush addressed the nation on the day after the bombing began, 61 million TV households were tuned in. It was the biggest U.S. audience for a single event in TV history.

Polls showed that four out of five Americans approved of the decision to attack Iraq. The United States was awash with patriotism, symbolized by flags flying and yellow ribbons displayed at homes and offices.

There was plenty to cheer about. The bombings shattered Iraq's air force in eight days; its planes were fleeing to neighboring Iran, its air defenses a shambles.

Next came the land war and another devastating victory that happened faster than anyone expected. When the Gulf War ended, fewer than two hundred allied men and women had been killed in action. Iraqi losses were estimated at a hundred thousand.

In only forty-three days, the U.S. had drawn on its technological superiority to spearhead one of the most decisive victories in military history. It defeated the world's fourth largest army of more than a half million troops, on which Hussein had lavished more than 60 billion dollars for arms between 1980 and 1988.

For the tens of millions of Americans who were glued to their TV sets, there was an overwhelming sense of relief. At one point, the U.S. government had predicted a war that could last four months. A week after it started, half of those polled expected at least five thousand Americans to die in combat. The Gulf War turned out to be only one thousand hours of fighting in the air and one hundred hours of air-land fighting.

One particular scene demonstrated the power of a single event to capture the story of victor and vanquished when TV cameras showed Iraqi soldiers falling on their knees and kissing the hands of U.S. Marines who had captured them.

The victory created a new military hero, General H. Norman Schwarzkopf, commander of Operation Desert Storm. A gruff, heavyset, no-nonsense West Pointer with a chubby face, he was a hit on television where he was known as "Stormin' Norman." As U.S. ground forces swept to success, Schwarzkopf gave a celebrated TV briefing on what happened. In *Unsilent Revolution,* a penetrating analysis of television news, Robert J. Donovan and Ray Scherer commented that "for fascinating narrative and clarity" his briefing "probably has no parallel in the history of television."

Not since the heroes of World War II, Generals Dwight D. Eisenhower and Douglas MacArthur, had a military leader reached such heights of fame and adulation. None had achieved it as quickly as the Gulf War hero, thanks to television. Schwarzkopf's overnight popularity paid off immediately: he retired after the war and earned about $8 million in his first year of retirement, including a $5 million book advance. (It would have taken him seventy years to earn that much on his $113,000 annual army salary.)

Both sides in the war used TV to send each other messages and strengthen their case with the worldwide audience. In Baghdad, Arnett was taken to sites where U.S. bombs fell so he could report on civilian damage and casualties. Saddam Hussein, a regular viewer of CNN, gave Arnett a special interview that enabled Iraq to get its point of view across.

The U.S. government used televised military briefings to keep its goals before the public and to send messages to the Iraqi government. In his autobiography, Schwarzkopf stated that in his press conferences he took into account the fact that "Saddam and his bully boys were watching me on CNN in their headquarters."

Lieutenant General Thomas E. Kelley, who became a celebrity after conducting televised Pentagon briefings, said he took into account the fact that Iraq's leaders were watching. He made a point of including warnings about any use of chemical weapons: he "wanted those guys to hear that."

U.S. Secretary of Defense Richard B. Cheney called the TV coverage "just one tremendous piece of adver-

tising for the United States military and for the people who serve in it."

The coverage also mirrored the important role of African Americans and women in the armed forces. African Americans were prominent both at the battle-front and at the Pentagon. The highly visible chairman of the Joint Chiefs of Staff, General Colin Powell, was an African American. During the Gulf War, Powell became almost as popular as the president.

Elizabeth Fox-Genovese of Emory University, an authority on women's studies, observed: "To see women performing well, with no drama or fanfare, seems to me to be more striking than anything else women have done lately. And because of television, it is written in the public consciousness now."

The U.S. military was determined to avoid what had happened in Vietnam when TV correspondents moved around freely and made the military leadership look bad. As in Grenada and Panama, it controlled media coverage and rationed the news.

Reporters were forced to cover the ground fighting by working in pools—small groups of reporters who covered the action and then shared their information with the other reporters. These pools, chaperoned by officers, were tightly supervised.

To keep reporters supplied with information, the U.S. military used skilled and savvy spokespersons. They knew the whole world was watching and were careful to avoid information that would help the enemy or embarrass the military. They provided army-produced videotapes that showed flawless bombing missions and did *not* show civilian casualties.

The celebrated CBS producer, Don Hewitt, summed

up "Operation Desert Storm" as "a television show. You know, *Showdown in the Gulf*. It sounded like [the movie] *High Noon*. It kind of cheapened us. It was a Super Bowl, but we were playing a bush league team." Author Kurt Vonnegut called it "history as entertainment."

What Americans saw on television made the U.S. military look not merely good, but great. The coverage built support for the war, the military, and the generals. A *Newsweek* poll found that almost 90 percent of Americans said they had "a great deal" or "quite a lot" of confidence in the military. Ten years earlier, it had been only 50 percent. Schwarzkopf's approval rating of 93 percent was even higher than the president's sky-high rating of 90 percent.

No one could argue with *Time* magazine's verdict: "The Pentagon did a masterly job of controlling coverage of the war."

For the U.S. military in general, a Pentagon spokesperson summed up the impact on TV-saturated Americans: "The stigma of Vietnam has been erased."

28

1990s EYE-OPENERS:

" WHAT I SAW MADE ME SICK "

THE BEATING OF RODNEY KING

On Saturday night, March 3, 1991, police cars with sirens screeching chased a speeding car and cornered it in a suburb of Los Angeles. When the African-American driver ran from the car, a police sergeant fired a 50,000-volt stun gun at him.

Then police officers took turns kicking and beating him with their clubs before arresting him. The driver, twenty-five-year-old Rodney King, suffered eleven fractures in his skull, a crushed cheekbone, a broken ankle, internal injuries, and possible brain damage.

Nearby, a thirty-one-year-old manager of a plumbing business, George Holliday, was trying out his new Sony camcorder. He heard the commotion and went out on the balcony of his second-floor apartment to videotape the scene, lit by the spotlight of a police helicopter.

That would have been the end of it, if Holliday hadn't contacted KTLA, a local station, and sold them the tape for five hundred dollars. He set in motion a well-established

Image taken from amateur videotape by George Holliday of Los Angeles police officers beating Rodney King, March 3, 1991. Inset image taken from CNN videotape of Rodney King speaking to reporters c. May 1992. (Copyright © 1991, 1992 by Cable News Network. All Rights Reserved)

TV scenario: KTLA ran the videotape locally on Monday night. CNN picked it up the following day. Then CBS, NBC, and ABC joined in the national media blitz.

By June, almost everyone in the United States knew who Rodney King was and had seen Holliday's film of the beating. A nationwide poll found that within weeks the eighty-one-second videotape had reached almost four out of five Americans. The country shared President Bush's reaction: "What I saw made me sick."

The videotape made police violence toward minorities suddenly the most talked about problem in the United States and triggered a national debate. After the Rodney King beating, more than three-fifths of those polled thought that "a lot" or a "considerable" amount of police brutality was directed against minorities.

The repercussions went far beyond Los Angeles, where the police sergeant and the three police officers were charged with assault with a deadly weapon and "excessive use of force." Throughout the country, cities and counties investigated police procedures. The U.S. Justice Department began a nationwide review of complaints about police brutality during the previous six years.

The beating provided ammunition for civil rights activists who had been trying to bring this issue to national attention for decades. African-American demonstrators in Los Angeles carried the message on their signs: HELP NOW BEFORE IT'S MY TIME. . . . STOP POLICE VIOLENCE. . . . THE CAMERA DID NOT LIE.

Fourteen months later, a mostly white suburban jury acquitted the four police officers in spite of the videotape that was expected to guarantee conviction. Outrage over the acquittal set off violence in May 1992 that was compared to an earthquake. Hispanics and some whites joined African-American protesters in the deadliest U.S. riot in twenty-five years.

The nation's second largest city disappeared under billows of smoke. Entire blocks were set afire, buildings vandalized, stores looted. The eighty-one seconds of the King-beating video and its fifty-six videotaped blows led to seventy-two hours of rioting and mayhem. The death toll was forty-four, the injured two thousand, the damage more than a billion dollars.

A year later, justice had a second chance. The policemen were tried again, this time on federal charges of violating King's civil rights. (The earlier trial involved state charges of assault.) The sergeant in charge and the policeman who did most of the beating were found guilty. The other two were acquitted.

The videotape became one of the half dozen most widely watched clips in television history, and it had been made by an amateur rather than by professional journalists.

The "camcording of America"—as it was called—had opened the door to video vigilantes who used their cameras to record news events and expose wrongdoing. Sales of camcorders (a combination of video camera and tape recorder) jumped 29 percent in 1990. The buying rush repeated what happened in earlier decades—from the 1950s boom in TV buying to the VCR boom of the 1980s. By 1991 when George Holliday videotaped the Rodney King beating, more than 14 million Americans owned camcorders.

"After Rodney King, everyone with a video camera wants to be a George Holliday," commented retired Los Angeles Superior Court judge Robert Weil.

That's what happened. An Ohio woman on vacation in Texas videotaped a policeman clubbing a handcuffed man. In California, a gay man videotaped a neighbor harassing him. In Michigan, a man videotaped a group of girls assaulting a woman outside a Detroit luxury hotel. These incidents, like others around the country, ended up on local TV, evoking public outcry and prompting official action.

Light, inexpensive, easy to use, the camcorder makes everyone a potential journalist, able to produce newsworthy videos that command local, if not national attention. They give TV power to the people.

As early as 1991, *Newsweek* worried about what this meant for TV journalists. They were losing their monopoly. "What happens when anyone anywhere in the world has the power to be a TV reporter?" asked the magazine's TV analyst, Jonathan Alter.

In a special ABC report, narrator Ted Koppel had the answer: "The world is in the early stages of a revolution that it has barely begun to understand: Television has begun falling into the hands of the people."

29

1990s HEROES AND VILLAINS:

" IT WAS RIVETING, THIS O. J. STUFF. IT WAS ADDICTIVE . . . FABULOUSLY, DELIRIOUSLY, DIZZINGLY ENTERTAINING "

O. J. SIMPSON

Shortly after 1:00 P.M. Eastern Daylight Time on Tuesday, October 3, 1995, 150 million Americans, including President Bill Clinton, stopped what they were doing and went to the nearest television set. For ten minutes, *Newsweek* magazine reported, "the nation stood still."

Americans set aside their work and left their desks. They put off making phone calls, shopping, or buying and selling stocks. At airports around the country, they delayed getting on airliners. New Yorkers brought midtown traffic to a standstill as thousands of them crowded to watch a giant TV screen above a billboard in Times Square.

It had happened many times before in the history of television. TV was once again demonstrating its power to make the entire nation pay attention to a single event. This time it was the verdict in the murder trial of O. J. Simpson, lionized as a legendary football star and nationally known for his network sports commentary

O. J. Simpson is hugged by his attorney Johnny Cochran after being found not guilty of murdering his ex-wife Nicole and her friend Ronald Goldman, October 3, 1995. (Reuters/Archive Photos)

and rental-car commercials. He was a made-for-TV murder defendant, a celebrity accused of stabbing to death his former wife, Nicole Brown Simpson, and her friend Ronald L. Goldman on Sunday, June 12, 1994.

Shocking as it was, the double murder had little significance in and of itself. It didn't involve the assassination or fall of a national leader, the fighting of a war, the conquest of space, or the appointment of a justice to the highest court in the land. It had all the makings of a crime story that would have had a short and sensational life if it weren't for prolonged saturation TV coverage.

Television blew the story out of proportion for reasons that had much more to do with television than with the crime itself. For one thing, the rise of cable TV meant that NBC, CBS, and ABC were in competition not only with each other, but also with the news-hungry cable networks. As always, in television the name of the game was to get as large an audience as possible. From network news shows and news magazines to live coverage, in the 1990s TV was going all out to make news entertaining by making it dramatic. The public wanted news on the trial, and television gave the public what it wanted.

Given the right story, TV news can outdo entertainment shows, and the O. J. Simpson trial was such a story. The astute media observer Neal Gabler rightly pointed out in *TV Guide:* "It was riveting, this O. J. Simpson stuff. It was addictive . . . fabulously, deliriously, dizzyingly entertaining."

Nothing keeps the audience interested like uncertainty about how everything's going to turn out. Suspense is the lifeblood of TV, whether it is tomorrow's weather, the final score of a game, or the outcome of an election. It keeps the audience tuning in to see what happens next. The Simpson trial was nothing if not suspenseful. Every day brought new surprises.

The audience was not only viewers. It became a nationwide jury that actually knew more about the case than the courtroom jury. By law, the jurors were excluded from seeing the legal maneuvering by lawyers on both sides. But TV viewers saw it all. CNN and Court TV covered the trial live—a total of 630 hours on CNN.

In the first nine months of 1995, the TV networks devoted as much time to the trial as to the year's three next-biggest stories, including the Bosnian civil war. Looking back on the Simpson trial, CBS anchor Dan Rather criticized the fact that "it was easier to make room in our broadcasts for the O. J. Simpson trial than for the war in Bosnia." There was an obvious reason: CBS had to keep up with the competition.

By verdict time, TV had provided nine months of play-by-play coverage of courtroom proceedings as well as supplemental analysis by legal experts. The prosecution and the defense had called 126 witnesses in a trial that had lasted 372 days from jury selection to verdict. Courtroom grandstanding in front of the TV cameras by both prosecution and defense attorneys lengthened the trial, as the lawyers became instant television stars.

Appropriately, the O. J. Simpson live coverage began with a bizarre, slow-motion chase five days after the murders. Simpson had been scheduled to turn himself in to the police on Thursday, June 16, 1994. When he failed to appear, an all-points bulletin was issued for his arrest. The police located him Friday evening, and for two hours, a caravan of police cars followed a white Ford Bronco carrying Simpson and his close friend and former teammate Al Cowlings over sixty miles of Los Angeles freeways. More than a dozen police and TV news helicopters hovered above.

Throughout the slow-moving chase, the police kept a cautious distance, speaking to Cowlings on a cellular phone while Simpson threatened to kill himself. All along the way, spectators jammed overpasses and roads to watch the bizarre procession that ended in Simpson's arrest. At home, an estimated 95 million Americans tuned in.

What happened on NBC during the chase typified the sensational coverage that viewers take for granted. Millions were already watching the network's broadcast of the National Basketball Association play-off game between the New York Knicks and the Houston Rockets. NBC switched back and forth between the two live events, sometimes showing both at the same time on a split screen. Afterward, NBC anchor Tom Brokaw commented that he could not remember anything like it in his thirty years on television.

On November 7, 1994, Judge Lance A. Ito unleashed the full force of live television when he permitted a TV camera in the courtroom. More than a thousand reporters from the United States and abroad descended on the Los Angeles County Courthouse. Their makeshift newsrooms, erected in a parking lot, were dubbed "Camp O. J."

On January 24, 1995, the trial began. The prosecution set out to prove that during an unaccounted-for seventy-eight minutes, Simpson drove to his ex-wife's home and committed two brutal murders in a jealous rage. Years before, O. J. had been convicted of beating his wife. The prosecution asserted that his violent nature had led him from abusing his wife to killing her. But the murder weapon was never found, and there were no eyewitnesses. The defense argued that the evidence placing Simpson at the scene of the crime was improperly gathered and mishandled, even planted by a racist police department. They contended that the prosecution could not prove that Simpson was guilty beyond a reasonable doubt as required by the law.

Once the trial got under way, it was hard to turn away from the TV coverage—or to escape it. For daytime viewers, it was a real-life soap opera. Millions of them left behind their favorite shows to watch the real thing. CNN's audience for live coverage was six times greater than normal and the network charged eight times its usual rates for late afternoon ads.

One measure of the trial coverage's impact was the cost to U.S. employers, calculated by the Cambridge Human Resources Group in Chicago. By twelve months after the white Bronco chase, an estimated $27 billion in productivity had been lost because of time people spent discussing the case on the job.

As it progressed, the trial began to resemble a soap opera more and more, with each episode more melodramatic than the last. Nicole Brown Simpson's sister Denise sobbed on the witness stand as she described O. J. Simpson's abusive treatment of her murdered sister. On February 3, she testified that on various occasions he had humiliated her sister in public, and that he had slammed her against a wall and thrown her out of the house. At one point, Denise's eyes locked with Simpson's. He immediately turned his head away.

Detective Mark Fuhrman, a key prosecution witness, testified that he found incriminating evidence, a bloody leather glove, behind Simpson's house. It matched a glove found near the murder victims. In testimony beginning March 9, Fuhrman denied ever using racist language. On September 9, Fuhrman lost credibility: The jurors heard a taped recording of the detective using racial slurs.

Brian "Kato" Kaelin, Simpson's houseguest, recalled the evening of the murder in what ended up more like a performance than testimony. He said he returned from McDonald's with O. J. at 9:35 P.M. and didn't see him again until 11:15 P.M. This included the time of the murder and therefore was crucial in prosecutor Marcia Clark's case against O. J. Simpson. From his first day of testimony on March 21, a confused and evasive Kaelin faced tough questioning from Clark, who kept trying to pin him down. The *New York Times* described him as "rather childlike." Defense lawyer Robert L. Shapiro tried to turn the jury against the prosecutor for her rough questioning. When Shapiro asked Kaelin, "Does she [Clark] intimidate you at all?" Kaelin answered that her questions frightened him.

On June 15, everyone in the courtroom leaned forward when prosecution lawyer Christopher Darden asked O. J. Simpson to put on the bloody glove found at the scene of the crime. "Too tight, too tight," the jury heard Simpson mutter as he struggled to pull on the glove. After the day's session, Simpson's chief defense lawyer, Johnnie Cochran, rejoiced in what he called a strategic mistake by the prosecution. "What the jury saw was that Mr. Simpson couldn't put those gloves on because they're too small. . . . There's no two ways about it."

Finally, at the end of September, the trial drew to a close, and the prosecution and defense made their closing arguments. After citing a series of laboratory tests from blood, hair, and fiber to put Simpson at the scene of the crime, prosecutor Marcia Clark finished with the recorded sounds of Nicole Brown Simpson's frantic telephone calls to the police. Nicole was heard sobbing as she reported abuse at the hands of O. J. Her sisters Denise and Tanya put their fingers in their ears to block the sound.

After arguing that Simpson could not have committed the murders in the time frame cited by the prosecution, defense attorney Cochran delivered a fiery summation. He squeezed into a pair of gloves to argue that the incriminating bloody glove did not belong to Simpson because it didn't fit. He kept saying, "If it doesn't fit, you must acquit." Cochran reminded the jury—nine of them black—about how often the criminal justice system fails African Americans. He charged that a bungling, racist Los Angeles police department had tainted the prosecution evidence and suggested that O. J. Simpson had been framed because he was African American. The idea of a police conspiracy seemed incredible to most whites. But many blacks remembered that this was the same police department that had brought national condemnation on itself for the shocking beating of Rodney King.

Race was a significant factor in how Americans viewed the Simpson trial. The nationwide jury of viewers was divided sharply along racial lines. Even before the trial began, a Gallup poll found that 68 percent of whites

said that Simpson was guilty, whereas 60 percent of African Americans said he was innocent. A subsequent NBC poll found that only 2 percent of African Americans would convict Simpson of first-degree murder. Only 15 percent would support even a second-degree-murder verdict. Fifty-nine percent believed he should be acquitted. The majority of white TV viewers believed he was guilty. *Newsweek* reported America was "a nation divided more than ever by the shades of its skin."

As the case went to the jury, the media predicted a lengthy deliberation. But after a trial that lasted nine months with 126 witnesses, 1,105 pieces of evidence, and forty-five thousand pages of transcript, the jury of ten women and two men, who had been sequestered for 266 days, reached its verdict in less than four hours.

Late in the afternoon on Monday, October 2, Judge Ito set the scene for the ten minutes that brought the country to a standstill. He had promised lawyers on both sides that he would give them four hours' notice before the verdict was announced. The nation had to wait until the next day to learn what the jury had decided so quickly.

It was live television to the end. At 10:00 A.M. Pacific Time, Deirdre Robertson, Judge Ito's law clerk, read the verdict: "We, the jury in the above-entitled action, find the defendant, Orenthal James Simpson, not guilty of the crime of murder."

There were gasps, sobs, outbursts of grief and anger. "Oh, my God," exclaimed Simpson's oldest daughter, Arnelle. His son, Jason, held his head in his hands and wept. Ron Goldman's father cursed under his breath. The range of emotional responses in the courtroom was mirrored throughout the country. The media recorded reactions in restaurants, bars, beauty salons, health clubs, churches, offices, and schools that demonstrated how differently whites and African Americans regarded the trial. One TV network showed a group of African-American law students at Howard University as the verdict was being read. They screamed and danced for joy, a reaction that shocked the majority of white viewers who had judged Simpson guilty.

An African-American political scientist at the University of Chicago, Michael Dawson, concluded: "Many whites are extremely saddened by what they've seen. . . . They're mystified—how can a murderer possibly be a hero?"

The entire Simpson episode demonstrated how TV transforms the object of its attention. TV was more than an open window through which Americans could watch a murder trial. TV acted as a magnifying glass, making an isolated crime seem momentous. In addition to the live coverage, the continual analysis and "expert" commentary on network news and talk shows kept the trial constantly before viewers. It forced Americans to think about race relations, domestic violence, and the criminal justice system. The trial raised hard questions. Is the criminal court system rigged against African Americans? Do the police and the courts downplay violence against women by the men in their lives? Can millionaires get away with murder because they can afford high-powered attorneys?

TV put all these issues under its magnifying glass, but most of all, it focused attention on how differently whites and blacks feel about the justice system and the way that African Americans are treated in U.S. society. Race made a difference in how they viewed the verdict.

A poll sponsored by *Newsweek* magazine found that 85 percent of African Americans agreed with the jury's verdict of not guilty, and 80 percent thought the jury was fair and impartial. On the other hand, most whites (54 percent) disagreed with the not-guilty verdict, and only 50 percent thought the jury was fair and impartial.

Amid the avalanche of commentary on the O. J. story, the comment of Harvard Law School professor Randall Kennedy went to the heart of the matter: "The O. J. Simpson trial, his acquittal, reactions to it and reactions to the reactions have revealed a racial division in our society more stark than most of us could have ever imagined."

30

INTO THE NEXT CENTURY:

" THE GLOBAL VILLAGE "

he prediction of 1960s media pundit Marshall McLuhan has become a reality. The world is a "global village" where news and information, as well as entertainment, are a worldwide, all-at-once, experience.

Television continues to evolve. The next technological generation is the telecomputer—a personal computer and a telephone, merged with a television set—which gives viewers control of what they see and when they see it.

Interactive television enables viewers to pick and choose not only what they watch, but what media they use—videotape, CD-ROM, on-line services, the Internet, or traditional broadcast TV. Instead of a communal experience, TV is becoming custom-made for the individual.

Sam Zelman, who helped lead CNN to its global status, paints this picture of TV news on his crystal ball: "You'll see people punching up individual stories to see and hear, as if they were turning pages in a newspaper. Somewhere, in some central core of the local cable

company, there will be tiny reels of tape with thousands of accumulated stories. You press a button, like on a jukebox, and your selection of a story comes up."

On one hand, television viewing around the world will become an infinite number of individual choices.

On the other hand, television will have the power to create a single audience, all watching the same major event at the same time, not just in the United States, but all over the world.

The worldwide audience is already here. Since 1980, the number of sets in the world has tripled to 1 billion, with the largest proportion in Europe (35 percent) and Asia (32 percent). Each year until the end of the century the number of sets is expected to increase by 5 percent (twice that rate in Asia).

All these televisions are linked by three hundred satellite-TV stations, with another seventy satellites to be launched by 1997. Satellite transmissions can bring hundreds, even thousands, of channels into homes everywhere on the globe. Worldwide, there is a rise in spending on TV programming to supply the demand: 80 billion dollars in 1993, increasing by 10 percent each year.

The United States is leading the world in a news and information binge. TV is filled with local and network news shows, news magazines, current-affairs specials, and documentaries. Some cable channels are completely devoted to business, court cases, sports, travel, and weather, with new specialized channels appearing all the time. Moreover, it is likely that CNN will be joined by other twenty-four-hour, all-news cable channels. Meanwhile, the exciting new information superhighway is creating countless possibilities for the exchange of images and ideas traveling in cyberspace to home computers.

The outlook is for many more choices and opportunities to get news and information through seeing images, which is what television is all about. Images add emotional power to information as no amount of words can. This experience of seeing for ourselves accounts for the impact of television.

How will these new technologies change America's mind in the future? That remains to be seen. Although television can focus millions of viewers' attention on a single event, watching is an individual experience and an individual choice. In making our selections and interpreting what we see, it's important to know that how we relate to television has followed a familiar pattern from its earliest years. Technology changes, but human nature holds steady. People will always respond to the themes described in this book: confrontation, politics, war, heroes and villains, and eye-opening information.

Watch carefully and you will see these themes repeat themselves as they have in the first fifty years of television. So will the ways in which television influences us as individuals and as a nation. With this awareness, we can look ahead to a new century with our eyes open to a changing world and the screen that brings it all home.

FURTHER READING

ABOUT TELEVISION

Barnouw, Erik. *Tube of Plenty: The Evolution of American Television*. New York: Oxford University Press, 1975.

Bliss Jr., Edward. *Now the News: The Story of Broadcast Television*. New York: Columbia University Press, 1991.

Donovan, Robert J., and Ray Scherer. *Unsilent Revolution*. New York: Cambridge University Press, 1992.

Goldstein, Norm. *The History of Television*. New York: Portland House, 1991.

Marschall, Rick. *The History of Television*. New York: Gallery Books, 1986.

Matusow, Barbara. *The Evening Stars*. Boston: Houghton Mifflin, 1983.

Mayer, Martin. *About Television*. New York: Harper & Row, 1972.

Westin, Av. *How TV Decides the News*. New York: Simon and Schuster, 1982.

ABOUT THE DECADES
The 1950s

Cook, Fred J. *The Nightmare Decade*. New York: Random House, 1971.

Gorman, Joseph Bruce. *Kefauver: A Political Biography*. New York: Oxford University Press, 1971.

Halberstam, David. *The Fifties*. New York: Villard Books, 1993.

Life. "The U.S. Gets A Close Look at Crime." March 26, 1951, pp. 33-39.

Manchester, William. *The Glory and the Dream, Part III*. Boston: Little Brown, 1973.

Reeves, Thomas C. *The Life and Times of Joe McCarthy*. New York: Stein and Day, 1982.

Wills, Garry. *Nixon Agonistes: The Crisis of the Self-Made Man.* Boston: Houghton Mifflin, 1970.

The 1960s

Blum, John Morton. *Years of Discord: American Politics and Society, 1964-1974.* New York: Norton, 1991.

Halberstam, David. *The Best and the Brightest.* New York: Random House, 1972.

Lewis, Richard S. *The Exploration of the Moon.* New York: Quadrangle/New York Times Book Company, 1974.

Life. "Men on the Moon." August 8, 1969, pp. 18-29.

Manchester, William. *The Glory and the Dream, Part IV.* Boston: Little Brown, 1973.

Newsweek. "Road from Selma: Hope—and Death," April 5, 1965; "The Big March: On a Treadmill?" November 24, 1969; "One Giant Leap," July 28, 1969; "The '60s," December 29, 1969.

Time. "The Moon: A Giant Leap for Mankind." July 25, 1969.

Warren, James W. *Portrait of a Tragedy: America and the Vietnam War.* New York: Lothrop, Lee & Shepard, 1990.

White, Theodore H. *The Making of the President, 1960.* New York: Atheneum, 1961.

Wilford, John Noble. *We Reach the Moon.* New York: Bantam, 1969.

THE 1970s

Bernstein, Carl, and Bob Woodward. *All the President's Men.* New York: Simon and Schuster, 1974.

Hammond, Charles M. *The Image Decade: Television Documentary, 1965-1975.* New York: Hastings House, 1981.

Karnow, Stanley. *Vietnam: A History.* New York: Viking, 1983.

Michener, James A. *Kent State: What Happened and Why.* New York: Random House, 1971.

Newsweek. "Putting Watergate Behind Us," Special Issue, August 19, 1974; "The Legacy of Richard Nixon," May 2, 1994.

Time. "Epitaph for a Decade." January 7, 1980.

White, Theodore H. *Breach of Faith: The Fall of Richard Nixon.* New York: Atheneum, 1975.

White, Theodore H. *The Making of the President, 1972.* New York: Atheneum, 1973.

Wicker, Tom. *One of Us: Richard Nixon and the American Dream.* New York: Random House, 1991.

THE 1980s

Cannon, Lou. *Reagan.* New York: Putnam, 1982.

Hohler, Robert T. *I Touch the Future: The Story of Christa McAuliffe.* New York: Random House, 1986.

Johnson, Haynes B. *Sleepwalking through History: America in the Reagan Years.* New York: Norton, 1991.

Lewis, Richard S. *Challenger: The Final Voyage.* New York: Columbia University Press, 1988.

Newsweek. "We Mourn Seven Heroes." February 10, 1986.

O'Shaughnessy, Hugh. *Grenada: An Eyewitness Account of the U.S. Invasion and the Caribbean History That Provoked It.* New York: Dodd, Mead, 1984.

Rose, Tom. *Freeing the Whales: How the Media Created the World's Greatest Non-Event.* New York: Carol Publishing Group, 1989.

Time. "Anybody Want to Go to Grenada?" November 14, 1983; "They Slipped the Surly Bonds of Earth to Touch the Face of God," February 10, 1986; "State of Siege," May 29, 1989; "China's Dark Hours," June 12, 1989; "Defiance," June 19, 1989.

Wells, Tim. *444 Days: The Hostages Remember.* New York: Harcourt Brace Jovanovich, 1985.

Wills, Garry. *Reagan's America: Innocents at Home.* Garden City, N. Y.: Doubleday, 1987.

Allen, Thomas B.; F. Clifton Berry; and Norman Polmar. *War in the Gulf.* Atlanta: Turner Publishing, 1991.

Baker, Russell. "The '92 Follies." *The New York Times Magazine,* November 1, 1992.

Binaculli, David. Chapter 17, "The Civil War to the Gulf War." In *Teleliteracy: Taking Television Seriously.* New York: Continuum Publishing Company, 1992.

Facts on File. "O. J. Simpson Acquitted in Double Murder Trial; High-Profile Case Sparks Debate on Race," October 5, 1995, pages 725-727.

Germond, Jack W., and Jules Witcover. *Mad as Hell: Revolt at the Ballot Box.* 1992; New York: Warner Books, 1993.

New Republic. "Unreasonable Doubt? Simpson, Race & America," October 23, 1995.

Newsweek. "Brutality on the Beat," March 25, 1991; "The Siege of L.A.," May 11, 1992; "The Verdict," October 16, 1995.

Phelps, Timothy M., and Helen Winternitz. *Capitol Games: Clarence Thomas, Anita Hill and the Story of a Supreme Court Nomination.* New York: Hyperion, 1992.

Rosenstiel, Tom. *Strange Bedfellows: How Television and the Presidential Candidates Changed American Politics, 1992.* New York: Hyperion, 1993.

Time. "History as It Happens," January 6, 1992; "Law and Disorder," April 1, 1991; "Special Report: The Simpson Verdict," October 16, 1995.

TV Guide. "O. J.: The News as Miniseries" by Neal Gabler, July 30, 1994.

U.S News & World Report. "The 'New News' and the Old," July 27, 1992; "The Untold Story" [of Anita Hill and Clarence Thomas], October 12, 1992; "What Now? The Great Racial Divide," October 16, 1995.

INDEX

Entries in italics are from photos and captions.